WAYS TO LEAD

Henry H. Knapp III

PREFACE

I'm a former US Army Special Forces Team Leader. I've spent most of my time since I left the Army leading small teams of technical professionals in Europe, Asia, and the United States. I've led a number of teams that developed highly innovative, superbly reliable products.

The ideas in this book come from my experience leading teams and working with other team leaders. They've proven their value on the ground - in combat and in business.

None of the ideas in this book is subordinate to any of the others. Any of them can be useful to you if you make it your own. And if you learn to use even a few of the ideas in this book, you'll become a more effective leader, and a more effective follower as well.

HOW TO USE THIS BOOK

Each one-page chapter of this book presents one idea. I suggest that you read the first 28 chapters in order – from KEEP A JOURNAL through SAY GOODBYE KINDLY - before you start to skip around. Doing that will give you an overview of the approach that informs the book.

Several of the chapters contain references to the titles of other chapters. You can use the CHAPTER INDEX at the back of the book to find chapters by title when you're skipping around to follow those references.

To learn more about any of the ideas, you can explore the other sources of information about it that I've listed in REFERENCES BY CHAPTER at the back of the book. There, for each idea, you'll find a list of references under the chapter title for the idea. The ANNOTATED BIBLIOGRAPHY contains more detailed information about each reference listed in REFERENCES BY CHAPTER, including information on where to find it.

If you think one of the ideas could be useful to you, test it by using it. I'll show you how to do that in HOW TO TEST AN IDEA. If the results of your tests indicate that the idea is in fact useful, practice using it until using it becomes second nature.

To get the full benefit of an idea, you need to change your behavior to incorporate it. To do that you have to practice the new behavior over and over until it becomes automatic.

It's quite easy to read a book, and even enjoy it, without testing or practicing the ideas it presents. If you find yourself doing that, lay the book aside for a while. Come back to it when you feel ready to work on improving your leadership skills.

KEEP A JOURNAL

To benefit most from the experiences this book will lead you through, you'll need to keep a journal. Reviewing your experiences from the vantage point of your later understanding will greatly increase their value to you. A journal is a wonderful aid to that process.

Keeping a journal is also a good way to get a better understanding of your own thoughts and feelings. Writing them down often clarifies them as nothing else can.

A simple computer text file will work as a journal. So will a ruled notebook.

The best way to keep a journal is to use it to write down as much as you can of what you experience. Notes on the ordinary events of the day can be just as useful as accounts of emotional or intellectual revelations. Don't censor yourself. You'll be glad you didn't.

Date each journal entry. That way when you reread your journal you'll be able to connect what you wrote to what was happening in your life when you wrote it.

You can start small. Promise yourself that you'll sit down for a few minutes each day and write. Don't worry about what or how much you write, and don't worry if you miss a day or two now and then. Just do it whenever you remember that you want to. The more you do it, the more you'll want to do it, but only if you start today and keep going.

Be careful not to give access to your journal to anyone else - not even your partner or your closest friends and associates. If your journal isn't completely private it won't be very useful to you, because you'll censor yourself as you write in it.

WHY LEAD?

Let's suppose for the moment that you're reading this book because you want to become a more effective leader. Here are some questions that may help you find your reasons for wanting to learn more about how to lead. Before reading any farther, get out your journal or open a file on your computer and write down your answers to them. You're writing for yourself, so just jot down the first thoughts that come to you. There's no need to pretty them up.

Have you found yourself leading a team or a group of people without having started out by intending to do that? If so, write down a few notes about how it happened.

Have you ever sought a leadership position? If so, write down a few notes about that experience. Include the reason you wanted the position, and what happened as a result of your efforts to get it.

Do you think you need to lead people in order to achieve your personal goals? If so, make a list of those goals, and write down your reasons for thinking that you need to lead people to achieve them.

Do you have other reasons for wanting to learn to lead? If so, list them now.

YOU MAY ALREADY BE A LEADER

One person can make the difference between success and failure for an entire team. Often that person isn't the official team leader. Sometimes only a few people know that that person is actually leading the team. Sometimes even that person doesn't know it.

People often get into leadership positions because they're good at doing at least one important task that their team needs to do. So if you're good at doing at least one of your team's important tasks, you'll quite likely find yourself leading the team sooner or later, at least for a while, regardless of your official position.

If you've acquired a valuable skill you'll likely wind up leading a team whose work requires that skill. That won't qualify you to lead the team, but it will help you get qualified.

BORN LEADERS, MADE LEADERS, AND FOLLOWERS

You probably know one or two people who seem to be born leaders. They attract leadership roles and know what to do in difficult situations. People naturally turn to them for advice and encouragement.

Most of us aren't born leaders. We get frustrated when we try to get other people to do what we think should be done, and we sometimes wonder if we should be leading at all.

However, all of us can learn how to lead better, and learning how to lead better will help us follow better when someone else is leading. You can test that idea by testing some of the other ideas in this book. If those ideas help you become a better leader and a better follower, then you'll have verified that people who aren't born leaders can become better leaders, and by doing so can become better followers.

And even born leaders can always learn how to lead better.

DO WHAT YOU WERE MADE TO DO

There's almost sure to be some part of every kind of work that you won't like doing. But if you don't like doing the most important things that you have to do at your work, you need to find another line of work.

In particular, you may be find that a leadership role doesn't suit you. There's nothing wrong with that.

America's obsession with entrepreneurs and business leaders distorts American thinking about success. Success isn't running a big organization or making a lot of money. Success is being able to make a decent living doing something useful that you enjoy. That can be almost anything - really, almost anything.

Do what you were made to do. That may mean that you have to make a career change. You can do that - and you'll be glad you did. You'll find help for making the change in the references for this chapter.

DO THE LITTLE THINGS WELL

You need to do your best every day to be good at what you do. That isn't easy.

Doing your best requires attention to detail. To do the big things well you need to do the little things well.

The way to do that is to keep improving at doing the little things. Watch yourself as you do the little things you do each day while doing your work. Look for opportunities to improve the ways you do those things.

Working on improving the ways you do the little things will get you working on improving the ways you do the bigger things. In fact, the bigger things are just collections of little things.

PIGHEADED DISCIPLINE AND DETERMINATION

Learning how to do anything takes effort. Learning how to lead may be harder than learning how to do almost anything else, though, because it involves learning how to get along with people – perhaps the most complicated creatures on the planet.

In the introduction to *The Ultimate Sales Machine,* Chet Holmes, one of the most influential leadership trainers in America, says that making the improvements he suggests takes pigheaded discipline and determination.

Learning how to use the ideas that this book presents also takes pigheaded discipline and determination.

SOME THINGS WILL HAVE TO GO

It's great to want to acquire new habits and skills that will make you better at what you want to do, but how will you find the time? Your days are already full, right?

Right. So some things will have to go. You'll have to break at least some of the habits that are holding you back.

There's a secret weapon for breaking habits. It's called substitution. You can't just stop a behavior without substituting another one. To stop indulging in a habit you want to get rid of, substitute another behavior.

Here's an example: Maybe you like to eat ice cream, and you're gaining weight because of that habit. Substitute a healthy low-calorie snack food like carrots or fruit, and keep a supply handy for when you're tempted to eat ice cream.

Another example: Maybe you have a tendency to look for objections to other people's ideas instead of looking for ways to make them work. Instead of looking for objections, try looking for advantages. Objections are easy to find. Try looking for ways to overcome the objections that you see.

Substitute more effective behaviors for behaviors you want to stop.

TAKE CARE OF YOURSELF

To do anything really well, you need to be at your physical, mental, and emotional best. World-class athletes do whatever they can to keep their bodies in top physical condition, and many of them also consult with sports psychologists to learn how to get into the right frame of mind for competition.

Treat yourself like a world-class athlete. Exercise. Eat right. Study Yoga or Qigong. Take up a gentle martial art like Aikido or Tai Chi.

Do things that put you in the right frame of mind to enjoy yourself and be productive. Find activities and rituals that relax and renew you. Work to stay healthy in body, mind, and spirit.

BUILD A PERSONAL SUPPORT TEAM

No one does it alone. The myth of the lone hero is just that – a myth.

You need people around you who can help you when you're having trouble. And you need people to help you do what you don't know how to do and don't have time to learn how to do.

You need an expert, compassionate personal physician. You need an expert, compassionate personal counselor. You need an expert dentist. You probably need an expert auto mechanic, handyman, insurance agent, banker, lawyer…

Start with your friends. Help them, and don't be shy about asking them for help.

Ask your friends to recommend professionals who can do the things that you can't do well. Use the rating services on the Internet, get referrals from other professionals, and get referrals from wherever else you think you can get unbiased recommendations.

Try to find several professionals who provide each service and get high marks from your referral sources. Interview them. Try them out. If one of them doesn't work out, move on to the next one on the list.

Remember, you're hiring them to be members of your personal support team. They're as important to you as the members of the team you work with.

When you find a good professional, do them and your friends a favor: tell your friends about them.

FIND MENTORS

Whenever you're learning a new skill, find at least one person who's mastered it and ask them to be your mentor and help you learn it. You can find a mentor for any skill you want to learn.

You can probably find more than one. That would be good.

A mentor can help you avoid wasting time pursuing activities that won't help you learn what you want to learn. A mentor can also help you avoid many of the pitfalls you might otherwise fall into while learning the skills that they've mastered.

Look for leadership mentors among the leaders you know and admire. When you've found one, tell them what you want to learn, ask for their help, and do what they suggest.

You'll want to offer them something they want in exchange. Be creative. It doesn't have to be money. Maybe you'll take a class from them. Maybe you'll buy a book they've written. Maybe you'll do both. Maybe neither. Ask them.

SPEND YOUR TIME WISELY

To make progress toward your goals, you need to make sure that every day you complete tasks that further your progress. A friend once told me that he feels he's doing well if he can work three hours a day on creative tasks. So do I. There's usually too much going on in our lives for us to be able to dedicate more than three hours a day to creative work.

But - and this is a big 'but' - you need to know what's most important to you, and spend as much of your time as you can doing that. Use to-do lists: when you think of a task that you need to complete to achieve one of your goals, put it on a to-do list. You can keep one to-do list for routine tasks, one for projects you're working on, and one for personal goals.

Divide large projects into tasks that can be done in an hour or less. Order the tasks on the lists by priority – the most important tasks go to the tops of the lists.

Don't try to list all the tasks that need to be done to achieve a goal. List as many as you can think of and add more as you think of them. Every day, review the to-do lists, remove tasks that you've finished, and reorder the remaining tasks as your priorities shift.

Every day, choose three tasks from your to-do lists that will further your progress toward your most important goals and make sure you get them done. Choose the tasks on the tops of your lists.

If you discover that you aren't finding enough time to work toward your most important goals, figure out why and fix the problem. The references for this chapter can help you learn how to do that.

BE AT YOUR BEST FOR THE HARDEST TASKS

Find the time of day when you're at your best, and use it to work on the tasks that require your best energy and intelligence.

I'm at my best in the early morning. I find it hard to get myself to exercise, so I exercise right after I get up in the morning.

I enjoy being with other people, so I don't need to reserve a special time for doing that. But I do need to reserve a special time for exercising.

You may find it harder to interact with other people than to work alone. If that's the case, here are two suggestions:

1. Reserve time when you're at your best for interacting with your teammates.
2. Seriously consider whether it's right for you to seek out leadership positions. People who prefer to work alone can be excellent leaders, but I think the best leaders enjoy the company of others more than they enjoy being alone.

KEEP YOUR PROMISES TO YOURSELF

The most important promises that you make are the ones you make to yourself. They're also the most difficult to keep. No one else may know when you break a promise to yourself. But you'll know.

Every time you break a promise you make to yourself, you weaken your will and make it easier to break it again. So be careful what you promise to yourself, and make sensible plans and arrangements to help yourself keep your promises. The references for this chapter can help you learn how to do that.

Finally, if you break a promise you've made to yourself, don't waste time and energy feeling bad about it. Figure out what went wrong, LEARN FROM MISTAKES, and figure out how to keep the promise in the future. Then move on.

AVOID HIERARCHIES

Official hierarchies exist because their leaders can't think of any better way to organize large groups of people. Official hierarchies are, by their very nature, clumsy and bureaucratic.

Communication between different groups within hierarchies is often slow and prone to error. As a result, the leaders of official hierarchies are often saddled with organizations that can respond only slowly and clumsily to their efforts to lead.

The leaders of hierarchical organizations also tend to promote subordinates whom they like. Unfortunately, the ability to please one's superiors isn't necessarily accompanied by creativity or the ability to lead.

When an official hierarchy is working well, it's probably because its members are ignoring the official chain of command and working directly with whomever they need to work with to get the work done.

The references for this chapter present some alternatives to hierarchies.

SOME LARGE ORGANIZATIONS WORK

Some organizations remain effective even as they grow to large size. Those organizations are almost always composed of many small organizations that communicate effectively with each other.

Such organizations motivate their members and coordinate their activities by persuasion rather than coercion, and depend on the democratic functioning of the small teams within them to get their work done.

The small organizations aren't hierarchies. They're teams of equals in which the person most qualified to lead the team for each task assumes the leadership quite naturally, and relinquishes it equally naturally when it becomes clear that another member of the team is better qualified to take the lead on the next task.

The leaders of large organizations composed of many small teams don't give orders to be passed down a chain of command. They set the overall direction of the organization, and persuade the organization's members to follow it by showing them that it's the right direction. Those kinds of leaders also build organizational cultures that support the flexible leadership structures of the many smaller organizations within the larger organizations. They do that by demonstrating a democratic leadership style in their own behavior and using the methods described in the references for this chapter.

EFFECTIVE TEAMS ARE PRECIOUS

Effective teams can accomplish much more than individuals working in hierarchies. It takes a long time, possibly years, to build an effective team.

When you've built an effective team, do everything you can to preserve it. Effective teams are precious.

SMALL IS BEAUTIFUL

The best size for a team is the smallest group of people that can reach the team's goals. Don't add anyone to your team unless you're sure you're going to need them to get the job done.

There were (and maybe still are) about 150 people on the Skunkworks team at Lockheed-Martin Aerospace Systems. That team could produce a working prototype of a revolutionary aircraft in 90 days or less. They did it several times in a row. In this age of extreme automation, your team can probably be much smaller than that and still produce excellent work.

BUILD YOUR TEAM WITH CARE

Make no mistake about it. Your team is a family.

Remember that when you're considering adding a new teammate. Give everyone on the team a chance to get to know every prospective teammate well before you add him or her to the team, and give everyone on the team the right to veto proposed additions.

Keep inviting people to visit and talk with the team about what they do and what you do, even when you're not looking for new teammates – indeed especially when you're not looking for new teammates.

Arrange the longest trial period you can – at least six months. That way, if the person doesn't fit in, you've made no long-term commitment to each other, so the separation will be relatively painless.

It's common practice for companies to hire people first as contractors, and only later as regular employees if they've done well as contractors. That's an intelligent way to build teams.

Get the team together to evaluate prospective teammates. Just remember that a prospective teammate is a person like you. Be respectful, perhaps especially so, when you talk about inviting them to join the team.

Keep a list of people you'd like to work with. That list will come in handy if you need to add a teammate on short notice.

TEST PROSPECTIVE TEAMMATES

When you're considering working with someone, arrange to test them. Ask them to help you with something small, or suggest that they try a new way to do something. Think of something for them to do that requires them to make a small effort. Then watch.

Don't ask them how they did or how their experiment went. Don't check up on them at all.

If they tell you that they did what you asked or tried what you suggested, ask them to do something else, or suggest that they try something else that requires a little more effort. Then watch again.

A few repetitions of such tests will tell you whether you'll enjoy working with them.

I do a fair amount of consulting these days and I qualify potential clients in the way I've described. When a potential client tells me they want to improve their business, I suggest one change. Then I wait. If they make that change and ask for more advice, I suggest another slightly larger change, and wait again.

Pretty soon I have a very good idea of how serious that person is about improving their business. Time and again that approach has helped potential clients avoid wasting money on advice they couldn't take.

BUILD TRUST

It's vital to build and maintain trust within your team. People who trust each other can do amazing things together. People who don't trust each other can't do much of anything together.

You can't build trust overnight, and you need to work consistently, day in and day out, to maintain it. It's very easy to lose trust, and very hard to reestablish it after you've lost it.

To build trust and keep it, obey these golden rules:

1. Stay positive.
2. Tell the truth.
3. Respect everyone.
4. Do what you say you'll do.

The rules are simple, but obeying them requires constant effort. The next four chapters describe the nature of that effort in some detail.

STAY POSITIVE

Focus on the team's goals and possibilities. Don't avoid talking about obstacles to success. Talk about how to overcome them.

Read AVOID EXPRESSING NEGATIVE EMOTIONS, and take a look at the references for that chapter.

When someone admits a mistake, be grateful. People only admit mistakes when they aren't afraid that they'll be blamed for them. Work with them to figure out why the mistakes were made and how to avoid them in the future.

Instead of criticising substandard results, help your teammates find ways to improve the team's performance.

When someone criticizes you, LISTEN. Then thank them. All you do if you object to criticism is make the person who criticized you reluctant to tell you about the next mistake they see you make.

If you have a strong difference of opinion with someone on your team, resolve it privately. If that doesn't work, get a third party – a skilled mediator who's not on the team – to help you. If you still can't resolve your differences, one of you may have to leave the team. Be open to the possibility that that person might be you.

TELL THE TRUTH

Telling the truth may seem simple, but it isn't. First you have to know the truth. Second, you have to use very precise language when you tell it.

To know the truth you need to have verified the facts you're reporting, either through direct observation or in some other reliable way. Then you need to report the facts as objectively as possible, neither sugar-coating nor overemphasizing unpleasant details.

If you're repeating what someone else said, something you read, or what you saw or heard in the media, you have to say so, and cite the source. And you can't report anything you saw, read or heard from one of those sources as fact.

If you're stating an opinion, say so. Don't report opinion as fact. Judgment of any kind, including praise, and especially criticism, isn't truth. It's opinion.

You can say what you think, or report what someone else said they think, or what they said they observed, but you need to make it clear that that's what you're doing. Otherwise you're stating opinion or hearsay as fact. It isn't.

RESPECT EVERYONE

You don't need to like everyone you work with, but you do need to respect them.

If you've built your team with care, everyone on your team has valuable skills that enable them to contribute to the team's success. Your job as the team's leader is to help each member of the team use their skills to help the team succeed. If you can do that, your respect for that person and that person's respect for himself or herself will grow.

Johann Wolfgang von Goethe, the eighteenth-century writer, statesman, and philosopher, advised his readers to treat everyone as if they're the best person that they can become. That's respect.

If you show respect to everyone you meet, almost everyone you meet will prove that they're worthy of it.

DO WHAT YOU SAY YOU'LL DO

You've probably already discovered that doing what you say you'll do is a lot harder than it sounds. Here are a few words about why that is and what to do about it.

To be able to do what you say you'll do, you need to be able to say what you cannot and will not do, especially when you know that your listeners won't like what they hear. So first get very clear about your values and limitations, then TELL THE TRUTH about what you can do, can't do, and won't do – even when you know that the person you're telling won't like what they hear.

You also need to plan. That means setting aside enough time to do what you said you would do, and allowing time for getting over the inevitable bumps in the road.

Finally, you need to pay the price. If you said you were going to do something, and it becomes inconvenient or even painful to do it, do it anyway. That's the only way to keep the trust of whoever expects you to do it.

MEASURE

How can you say you can or can't do something if you don't know how long it will take? And how can you know how long it will take if you haven't measured it, at least informally?

If you're a reasonably well-organized person, you already know how long it takes to get through your morning routine and get to work. If you're running late, you know which tasks to skip and how much time you'll save by skipping them. So you've already been measuring things, even if only informally.

You don't need to measure much more formally than that to have a good idea of how long it takes you and your teammates to do the things you need to do to get your work done. You just need to make the measurements and record them. You can do that in a few minutes a day if you develop a simple scheme for doing it.

When you've accumulated measurement data, you need to use it. Use it to plan, and use it to increase the effectiveness and efficiency of what you do.

Measuring the amount of effort and time it takes to do what you do can be very helpful. Measuring the quality of what you do can be even more helpful. The references for this chapter contain the information you need to do those things.

IT'S NOT ABOUT BEING A NICE GUY

It's about being honest and reliable, and not blaming your teammates for making honest mistakes or being the bearers of bad news. In other words, it's about building trust.

If you consistently avoid blaming teammates when they bring bad news or make honest mistakes, you'll soon see them working hard to show you the honesty and reliability that you demonstrate yourself.

SAY GOODBYE KINDLY

When someone leaves your team, remember that he or she is a member of the family who's leaving home. Maybe they're moving on to pastures they think are greener. Maybe they didn't fit in. The reason they're leaving doesn't matter. The mere fact that they're leaving means there will be at least a little suffering, for them and for the rest of the team.

Everyone who leaves your team should leave at least a little better off than when they joined it. Here are some ways to make that happen.

1. Do your best to lead them well while they're on the team.
2. Do whatever you can to help them find a team they can succeed with.
3. If they ask you, talk with them about how they can increase their chances for success on their next team.
4. Ask them what you and the other members of the team could have done to make their time on the team more successful and enjoyable.

DON'T MAKE EXCUSES

When something goes wrong and you're tempted to offer an excuse or an explanation, don't. Instead, just say you're sorry and that whatever went wrong won't go wrong again. Then LEARN FROM MISTAKES and do what it takes to make sure that it doesn't.

DON'T REACT - RESPOND

When you're in a difficult situation, don't react. Respond.

Take your time. Stay aware in the moment. Watch yourself as you let the anxiety, fear, irritation, or anger pass. Emergencies usually aren't as urgent as they seem to be.

You need to think about how to respond. You may need to get away from the situation for a while and calm down before you decide how to respond.

You can almost always say, "Let me think about that. I'll get back to you (later today, tomorrow, next week)."

You may want to ask someone you respect and trust for advice before responding.

Measure your response. Don't just react.

WE'RE ALL DOING OUR BEST

One of my favorite leadership trainers, and one of my mentors, Jerry Weinberg, describes what he calls "the helpful principle" in his book *The Secrets of Consulting.* The helpful principle states that everyone is trying to help, even though it may look as though they're trying to do the opposite.

I translate the helpful principle as follows: everyone is doing his best to get what he or she wants without needlessly injuring or interfering with anyone else. Most people simply don't seem to know how to do that.

In fact, most people don't even seem to know what they really want. They seem to think they want what society has told them to want. More importantly, most people don't seem to realize that it's completely unnecessary to injure or interfere with anyone else to get what you want, if what you want is possible.

People often seem to have distorted ideas of what's possible. They imagine that things are possible that are impossible, and imagine that things are impossible that are actually possible.

I once watched a manager try to impose an impossible schedule on a software development project. His efforts resulted in later delivery of the software than would have resulted from a more reasonable schedule, and almost completely destroyed the morale of the development team. The quality of the product was so poor that it needed extensive repairs long after the project was supposed to have been completed.

What causes people to injure and interfere with each other is ignorance - not malice or evil intent. They just don't know any better.

So if you see someone acting in a way that you think jeopardizes the team's success or injures someone, put it down to ignorance and see if you can find a way to help them overcome it.

AVOID EXPRESSING NEGATIVE EMOTIONS

Some people may have habits and character traits that irritate or anger you. Remember, other people weren't put on this planet to please you. They're in the same position as you and I. Neither they nor you nor I asked to be here.

Think about how you react to natural events. Do you get irritated on hot days? The heat can certainly be very irritating. Does the irritation help you cope with the heat?

A storm can inconvenience and even endanger you. Does it help to get resentful or angry at it?

Think about how you would react if a dangerous animal were chasing you. Would you get angry? Would that help you?

People are part of nature. Nature is neither good nor bad. It just is. Getting angry about it won't change it or help you live in it. Likewise, getting angry with other people won't change them or help you work with them.

The references for this chapter can help you learn how to avoid expressing negative emotions. Look especially at *Zero Limits,* by Joe Vitale and Hew Len.

APOLOGIZE, FIX IT, AND MOVE ON

The first thing to do when you realize that you've been doing something damaging is to stop doing it.

Above all, don't criticize yourself. That's a waste of time and energy. If you remember that WE'RE ALL DOING OUR BEST, you'll realize that you acted from ignorance rather than malice.

When you've injured or inconvenienced someone, admit your error. Apologize.

If they aren't in a position to hear your apology when you're ready to make it, apologize in your heart. As soon as they're in a position to hear your apology, say what's in your heart. If it may be a long time before you see them again, send them a note or an email message or call them on the telephone.

Feel your apology in your heart as you apologize to them. Often there's no need to do anything else.

If you think you need to do something to heal an injury that you caused, ask the person you injured. They know more about what they need than you do.

Fix the mistake in your memory so you won't repeat it. Repair the damage as best you can. Then move on.

DON'T HOLD GRUDGES

Grudges distort your judgment. Forgive the people who injure or inconvenience you.

But don't forget what they did . Remembering what they did will help you decide whether and how to work with them in the future.

Don't give in to the impulse to retaliate when someone injures you. Instead, AVOID EXPRESSING NEGATIVE EMOTIONS.

If you conclude that a person can't contribute enough to the team's success to justify continuing to work with them, SAY GOODBYE KINDLY. Otherwise, adjust your behavior toward them to take their character into account.

GIVE FEEDBACK

Positive feedback releases stored energy. Negative feedback provides control. Useful work requires the controlled release of stored energy. It therefore requires the use of both positive and negative feedback.

Too much positive feedback produces an uncontrolled release of energy – an explosion. Too much negative feedback produces paralysis.

One of the jobs of a team leader is to give feedback to the team he or she is leading. The leader needs to provide positive feedback by helping and encouraging the members of the team. He or she also needs to provide negative feedback by helping the team avoid actions that lead it away from its goals.

The team provides the energy and skill required to accomplish its goals. The leader provides guidance in the form of positive and negative feedback.

THE BEST LEADERS

The best source of positive feedback is a friend's encouragement. The best source of negative feedback is the wisdom that experience can provide. The best leaders are wise, experienced friends.

George Bernard Shaw said, "The only service a friend can really render is to keep up your courage by holding up to you a mirror in which you can see a noble image of yourself."

Hold that mirror up to your teammates. Befriend them. If you can't befriend every one of your teammates, one or more of you should leave the team. It won't be a disgrace if you're the one who leaves.

HAVE FUN

In general, it's a good idea to AVOID WORKING OVERTIME. There is one exception to that advice though: If you're having fun at what you're doing, you can work longer hours and still be effective.

Have fun with your teammates. During work. Outside of work. BRAINSTORM WITH YOUR TEAMMATES to come up with ways to have fun together.

Let your sense of humor show. Help everyone see the humor in the situations you encounter as you work toward your goals.

Long ago one of my friends said, "If you're not having fun, you're not doing it right." I agree.

MIX IT UP

Another way to stay fresh when you're working a lot is to mix your activities. Switch from sitting at a desk thinking and writing to an activity that gets you moving. Exercise. Go for a walk. Reorganize your office. Clean something.

Mingle with your teammates. Don't intrude, but spend some time each day hanging out informally with them, individually and as a group. If either you or they are working remotely, call them on the phone, exchange email messages with them, or chat with them on line. Encourage them to do the same themselves.

A Swiss software development team I was on for a while used to have tea together every afternoon. Some of our most creative solutions to problems emerged from the informal conversations we had during those tea breaks.

TAKE BREAKS

Don't work on any task more than 45 minutes without taking a break. Don't sit longer than 45 minutes at a time looking at a digital display. When I'm working I take breaks every 30 minutes or so and walk around or do something else physical for a few minutes to clear my head. Encourage your teammates to take breaks too.

You also need breaks if you're involved in prolonged physical activity like construction work. The U.S. Army requires that recruits in training get a 10-minute break every hour. They know what they're doing.

AVOID WORKING OVERTIME

There's good thinking behind the eight-hour workday. The Germans work fewer hours each week than almost anyone else, and they seem to be doing quite well. America's love affair with long working hours just shows that many of us don't have lives outside of our work.

The longer you work each day, the harder it is to stay focused and effective. I've often seen people damage or destroy the results of earlier work during the extra hours they worked when trying to finish a job quickly. Haste, which often involves working overtime, makes waste.

If you see that one of your teammates is putting in a lot of overtime, encourage them to find a way to stop. If they say that they don't see how to get their work done without putting in a lot of overtime, BRAINSTORM WITH YOUR TEAMMATES to find ways to reduce their workload.

TAKE TIME OFF

You need to get completely away from your work for extended periods – at least once, preferably twice, a year. In the United States few of us think we can afford to do that, and as a result we get stale and lose enthusiasm for our work.

When you feel yourself losing enthusiasm for your work, plan a vacation. Even a three-day vacation may be long enough to restore your pleasure in your work, but longer is better.

Some companies offer year-long sabbaticals to their more experienced employees. Often those employees return from their sabbaticals with fresh insights that they can apply to their work.

Universities commonly offer year-long sabbaticals to tenured professors. Important creative work has emerged from such changes of scene.

Vacations don't have to cost much, either. When money is really scarce you can take a STAYcation. Explore your own neighborhood, town, or city. Catch up on projects you want to finish at home. Read that book you haven't found time to read.

Encourage your teammates to take time off when they sense that they're losing enthusiasm for their work. Schedule projects to include time off for everyone.

DON'T TELL - ASK

Start by asking for help with small tasks. Don't ask for help with big tasks unless you really need it, and the person you ask has proven that they can do what they say they'll do.

Give them room to say no. Ask them if they think they have the time, and if they're sure their current work won't suffer. If they say they can't help you, don't press them.

If someone says they'll help you with something, don't check up on them to make sure they've done it. Wait for them to tell you that they've done it. You'll learn a lot about them that way.

You'll also get the benefit of a phenomenon called signing up. Tracy Kidder described it in his book *The Soul of a New Machine*. People on the computer system development team that he wrote about in that book would do whatever they could to complete every task they had volunteered to perform. They moved heaven and earth to get them done when they had said they would. They had signed up to do those tasks and they weren't going to let their teammates down. If you ask instead of telling and BUILD TRUST, the people on your team will work just as hard not to let you and each other down.

GET UNSTUCK

Whatever you're trying to do, at some point in the process you're going to get stuck. You'll get stuck many times as you learn how to lead.

Relax. That's normal.

To get unstuck, get completely outside the situation you're in. Take a break, take a walk, go do something else, sleep on it. If that doesn't work, get help.

Help can come in many forms: from a mentor, a friend, a teammate, someone on another team, this book, some other book, a website... Keep your eyes and ears open and ask around.

Brainstorming is a good way to get good new ideas, and one of the best ways to get unstuck. I'll show you how to do that in the next two chapters – BRAINSTORM BY YOURSELF and BRAINSTORM WITH YOUR TEAMMATES.

BRAINSTORM BY YOURSELF

Just start writing down your thoughts about the question or problem you're thinking about. I open an idea file on my computer and type my thoughts into it as they come to me.

Don't censor yourself. If an idea seems crazy or irrelevant, write it down anyway. An idea may come up that's quite relevant to the question you're trying to answer or the problem you're trying to solve, but it may be worded in a way that makes its relevance hard to see.

Be patient. If you keep writing out your thoughts, you'll eventually see the direction they're taking. They can take you to some really interesting places.

If you get a good idea, that's no reason to stop writing. There may be more where that one came from. Keep writing down ideas until you run out of steam. If no interesting ideas come, do something to GET UNSTUCK.

After you've generated some ideas that look interesting, choose the ideas you want to work on. Score each idea for three attributes:

1. Positive impact on the possibility of achieving the goal
2. Ease of implementation
3. Speed of effect

Give each idea a score of from 1 to 10 for each of the three attributes, then total the three scores for each idea.

Do the scores make sense? Are the ideas with the highest scores really the best ones? Are there any ideas that you need to implement to satisfy legal, safety, or other outside requirements? Use the answers to those questions to choose the ideas to work on.

BRAINSTORM WITH YOUR TEAMMATES

Group brainstorming works best when the size of the group is more than two and less than ten.

Ask everyone in the brainstorming group to brainstorm by themselves before the group meets to brainstorm, and write down their ideas on the subject in priority order, starting with the idea they think is best. Then get everyone together and go around the group, asking each person in turn to state one idea from his or her list, starting with the one they think is best. On the next round, ask people to state their second-best idea, and so on. Don't allow any discussion of the ideas.

Ask someone to summarize each idea in a few words on a flip chart or white board where everyone can see it. Make sure the person who stated the idea agrees that the written summary of the idea summarizes it accurately.

Keep going until everyone's ideas have all been written down. If someone runs out of ideas before everyone else, they can just pass when their turn comes around.

After all the ideas have been recorded, allow time for people to state new ideas that may have been stimulated by those they just heard. Go around the group again, again allowing people to pass if they don't have any more ideas. Keep going until no one has any more ideas.

Have everyone score the ideas the way I described in BRAINSTORM BY YOURSELF. Then discuss the scores. Do they make sense? Do people agree that the ideas with the highest scores are the best ones? Are there any ideas that have to be implemented because of legal, safety, or other requirements? Follow the discussion rules that I list in AGREE ON YOUR GOALS.

TEST NEW IDEAS

Don't assume that any new idea that you encounter is useful. Try to prove that it is by testing it in your work and in your personal life.

Never test an idea by trying to prove that it's not useful. That isn't a valid test. Try proving that it's useful instead. That way, if you conclude that it's not, you're pretty sure to be right. You may also discover surprising and valuable ideas that you would otherwise miss.

I'll show you HOW TO TEST AN IDEA in the next chapter.

HOW TO TEST AN IDEA

Start by assuming that the idea is useful.

State the idea in one or two sentences. Write your statement of the idea in your journal. Ask yourself what results you expect to get if you test the idea and it turns out to be useful. Add a statement of the expected results to the statement of the idea.

Test the idea for a limited period, but give yourself enough time to perform a thorough test. Set specific dates for the beginning and end of the test. Write them down in your journal. You may only need a week to test some ideas, while for others you may need months or even years.

At the end of each day of the test, record your observations in your journal. Did you use the idea? If so, what happened? Did using it produce the result you expected? Why? Why not?

Review your observations at the end of the test period. When evaluating the results of the test, be honest with yourself. Did you conduct a thorough test of the idea? If not, why not? Can you use what you learned by running the test to run a more thorough test?

If you conclude that the idea is useful, keep practicing it. Keep recording your observations. Keep it up until using the idea becomes second nature to you.

OTHER SOURCES OF IDEAS

REFERENCES BY CHAPTER lists at least one other source for each of the ideas in this book. You can, and should, go to those sources to learn more about how to use the ideas. You'll need to read about, think about, test, and use each idea many times in order to make it your own.

IGNORE USELESS IDEAS

Testing most of the ideas you encounter isn't worth your time. They may be very good ideas, but learning about them won't help you achieve your goals. So before you spend time and effort testing an idea, ask yourself whether it can be of any use to you. If not, forget about it and move on. Ignoring useless ideas can help you avoid wasting a lot of time and effort.

PRACTICE USING IDEAS THAT YOU FIND USEFUL

You need to practice using an idea that you find useful or you won't remember to use it at the right time. For example, this chapter presents the idea that the best way to learn how to use an idea is to practice using it. You probably agree with that idea. You may already realize that you usually don't remember ideas and skills that you don't use. But do you remember that realization when it would be useful to do so? Do you use it to acquire new knowledge?

Use this idea on itself. Test it. Try using it to learn other ideas that you want to learn to use. See if it helps you learn how to use useful ideas. If it does, you will have learned how to use a useful idea that will help you learn how to use other useful ideas.

To lead a team well, you need know how to do the work the team is doing. You don't have to be an expert at it, you don't even have to have the talent needed to do it well, but you do need to know how to do it.

If you're appointed to leadership of a team whose work you don't know how to do, you can learn how to do it from the team as your leadership evolves. In fact, that may be the best way to learn how to do it. Teaching you how they do the work will also help your teammates understand how to do it better.

Even if you're expert at the work the team is doing, you can always learn more about how to do it from your teammates. That's an excellent way to show your respect for them and earn their respect as well.

It's true that just knowing how to do the work won't make you a good leader. You need skills that enable you to encourage your teammates and help them keep moving toward your goals. But it makes no sense to try to lead a team that's building a house if you know nothing about building houses.

STAY FOCUSED

Christine Comaford, a skillful Internet marketer, once said, "If you see something shiny off to the side of the path to where you're going, don't go over there to look at it."

When I get an intriguing new idea, I open an idea file on my computer and write the idea into it. Then, if it appears to contribute to the achievement of one of my goals, I might put it on one of my to-do lists.

I have idea files for a number of possible projects on my computer. I may never have time to work on any of those projects. That's fine with me. I have plenty to do to finish the projects I've already started.

This idea might seem to contradict STAY FOCUSED, because it might tempt you to let yourself get distracted from the most important tasks you need to complete. However, sometimes the best way to minimize the time and energy you spend on a task is to do it as soon as you realize that it needs to be done. That can save you the time and effort it takes to put it on a to-do list, schedule time for it, and remember to do it.

It takes good judgment to avoid being distracted and still do those little things that need to be done. If you don't already have that good judgment, you'll develop it as you learn to use the ideas in this book.

KEEP EVERYONE INFORMED

Everyone on the team deserves to know everything known about the issues that affect the team and him or her personally. Make it your personal goal to keep everyone up to date on every issue in the work environment that could affect them.

Don't burden them with unnecessary detail. Blizzards of email about trivial issues numb the mind and bury essential information.

Do, however, keep them informed about every issue in the work environment that might be important to them.

STAY OUT OF THE WAY

In an ideal world, the team would set its own goals and achieve them without needing anyone to guide it or check on its progress. Get as close to that ideal as possible.

Help the team guide itself and check on its own progress. Ask questions, point out potential problems, and help the team set up a system for keeping track of progress. Then get out of the way.

If the team needs resources or advice, you can offer them, but it's best for the team, and for the organization it's working in, if the team members themselves learn to do as much as possible of what needs to be done.

DON'T SUGGEST SOLUTIONS

Resist all temptations to suggest solutions to problems. Instead, help the team find solutions. That shows respect.

Besides, the solutions the team comes up with will almost certainly be better than the ones you come up with yourself. Two or three or four heads are almost always better than one, and your teammates have probably been thinking about the problems much longer than you have.

Help the team learn new methods for solving problems. Start by learning to BRAINSTORM BY YOURSELF and BRAINSTORM WITH YOUR TEAMMATES. Then use the references for this chapter to learn more methods. Study those methods. Learn how to use them. They work.

AVOID UNNECESSARY MEETINGS

Good reasons for meetings:

1. To make decisions and solve problems
2. To develop trust, rapport, and esprit de corps

Bad reasons for meetings:

   Anything else.

You can track progress in any area by posting charts that show how you've been doing in that area over time. Post the charts in public areas, and on websites and electronic bulletin boards.

You can disseminate other information by posting it on websites and bulletin boards, or by sending it out via email.

Question-and-answer sessions can make good meetings if they build trust, rapport, and esprit de corps.

Celebrations are great for developing rapport and esprit de corps.

See if you can think of other reasons to have meetings, good or bad, and see if you can find more effective ways to get the results that the meetings are supposed to produce.

INVEST IN PROCESS IMPROVEMENT

You can't get better at what you do unless you make time and allocate resources for process improvement. Most of the big companies I worked at simply weren't able to improve the quality of their products or reduce their time to market or cost of production because they didn't make the time or allocate the resources needed to do that.

They were too busy carrying buckets of water to the fire to find the time to put fuel in the fire engine.

Don't let that happen to you.

Apply a simple investment model to your team's operation: spend ten percent of your time working on improving the way you do things.

That will be hard. When you're working on a project with a firm completion deadline you'll be tempted to steal time from your investments in improvements to work on that project. Don't do it. Find some other way to meet the deadline. Or renegotiate it.

KEEP IMPROVING THE WAYS YOU DO THINGS

If you're not improving, you're getting worse. Look for opportunities to improve everything you do – personally and as a team.

Focus on improvements that will have the most impact on your ability to achieve your goals. BRAINSTORM BY YOURSELF and BRAINSTORM WITH YOUR TEAMMATES to decide what to improve and how.

Keep it up. Don't stop. Ever.

POINT OUT WHAT NEEDS TO IMPROVE

Point out situations that need to improve. If the people you're leading notice that you're paying consistent, relentless attention to a situation that needs to improve, the situation will improve.

AUTOMATE ROUTINE TASKS

Take a look at the routine tasks you perform every day, and encourage your teammates to do the same.

To begin, pick one task that consumes a significant amount of time.

Write an outline of the steps required to complete the task. You can use a spreadsheet. Use the leftmost column for a short name for each step, and the next one for a short description of it. If completion of the task requires the work of more than one person, use the next column for the name or title of the person performing each step required to complete the task. Use the rightmost column for that step's duration. You now have a procedure for completing the task.

The next step is to analyze the procedure to see how it can be improved, shortened, or automated. Maybe only some of the steps can be automated, maybe none. It's almost certain, however, that the procedure can be improved and shortened.

BRAINSTORM WITH YOUR TEAMMATES to get ideas for improving and shortening it. You can create a new version of the procedure spreadsheet for each idea that you get for improving it. Evaluate the suggested improvements the way I describe in BRAINSTORM BY YOURSELF.

Then make the changes that make the most sense. MEASURE the results of the changes. Repeat the cycle until you're satisfied with the results the procedure produces.

BE CAREFUL HOW YOU ECONOMIZE

When you're tempted to skip steps in a process to speed it up, be careful. You may later find yourself spending more time cleaning up after yourself than you saved by skipping the steps. In most cases, if you take care to do a job right the first time, and check carefully to make sure that you have, you'll save time in the long run.

I've watched software development teams try to shorten project schedules by skipping technical reviews and testing, only to find themselves spending much more time than they saved, finding and fixing errors after they released the software. They probably would have found those errors earlier and with less work if they hadn't skipped those steps in the process.

Often "quick and dirty" becomes slow and broken.

MEASURE IMROVEMENT

Find a way to measure improvement in each thing you want to improve. Choose a time-span during which improvement is possible. Then make that time-span the interval over which you measure improvement. Don't miss a measurement interval. Display the measurements where everyone on the team will be sure to see them every day. Use charts and graphs to show the trends.

When you have the improvement you want, don't stop measuring and posting the results. You can probably do even better, and if you stop paying attention, you may start doing worse.

PLAN BACKWARD

When you're starting to plan a project or figure out how to reach one of your goals, work backward from the goal. Write down a short description of the final step in the series of steps that reaches the goal. Then write down a short description of the step that precedes it, then the step that precedes that one, and so on until you reach the starting point.

For big projects start at a high level, with big steps that you expect will take a minimum of a month's work by one person. You can do more detailed planning later if you need to.

Don't try to figure out whether you can perform two or more steps in parallel. Your planning tools can do that for you. Just write out the steps in reverse order. Include all the main tasks that have to be completed .

You'll then have the data you need to feed into a planning tool to plan the project or chart your way to your goal.

DON'T FALL IN LOVE WITH PLANNING TOOLS

Sometimes you need to use sophisticated planning tools to keep track of all the tasks you have to complete to achieve your goals. But - don't let the tools obscure the simple fact that in order to do things well, you need to remember why you're doing them.

Remember also that you're leading people - not "human resources", tasks on a task list, or progress bars on a Gantt chart. Use your planning tools to free up time for working with people.

USE THE RIGHT TOOLS FOR THE JOB

Meetings are tools for solving problems, making decisions, and building trust, rapport, and esprit de corps. Email, web pages, and bulletin boards are tools for disseminating information. Brainstorming is a tool for generating ideas and finding solutions to problems. This book presents you with over a hundred other tools.

What do you want to accomplish? Find the right tools for that purpose either here or elsewhere.

CHOOSE YOUR TOOLS WITH CARE

How do you choose a tool from a set of candidate tools of the same type, like three different brands of electric drill? Of course you need to compare them.

You can find a partial model for comparing tools in the Consumers Union's evaluations of consumer products in *Consumer Reports*. Take a look at how they do it, then try a similar procedure when comparing candidate tools for your own use.

First write out a functional specification. What should the tool do, and how should it do that? Don't put in a lot of detail. You're choosing a tool, not making it. The functional specification should, however, give you a list of attributes that the tool needs to have to do the job you want it to do in the way you want it done.

Gather data about each candidate tool. Find people who have used it and ask them how well it satisfies each of the requirements represented by the attributes you've come up with. You may have to test a borrowed or trial version of each candidate tool to get the information you need to evaluate it. Then use the Consumers Union comparison method or something similar to compare the candidate tools.

When you're done you should be pretty sure that you know which candidate tool is best for the job you want the tool to do.

GET THE BEST TOOLS YOU CAN AFFORD

Every job requires tools. Some are physical, like electric drills or chainsaws. Some aren't.

Books are tools. Websites are tools. Ideas are tools. Computer software is a tool. Education and training are tools.

You need good tools to do a good job. The individual team members need good tools, and the team as a whole needs good community tools. Make the time and allocate the resources to get and maintain the best tools you can afford.

At least one team member needs to take responsibility for acquiring and maintaining the team's tools. They can interview the other team members to find out what tools they're using, what tools they like, what tools they don't like, and what tools they think they need. They can promote discussion of tools among the team members, to make sure that everyone on the team knows what tools are available and can take advantage of the experience that other team members have with those tools. Make sure that everybody on the team gets the time and resources to do all of that.

DON'T GET FASCINATED BY TECHNOLOGY

There's a big difference between a gadget and a tool. A tool helps you do work that needs to be done. A gadget can be fascinating, but may not be able to help you at all.

Learn the difference, and remember it when you're spending your money on technology.

THERE'S NO SILVER BULLET

It would be great if there were one method that could assure a team of success in its endeavors – the proverbial silver bullet. Lots of people will tell you that no such thing exists... and then try to sell you one. Stay out of that market.

There's a reason that this book suggests so many ways to be a better leader. To be an effective leader you need to master as many of them as possible. There is no silver bullet.

The past and future are of almost no importance compared to the present. The present is the only time you can lead – or do anything else.

But what about right now? How can you lead right now? After all, you're probably alone while you're reading this book.

Just try to be here now, reading this book. Don't let yourself get distracted by random thoughts that may be running through your brain. Control your attention to keep it on the book. That's what you'll have to do to keep your attention on doing what you need to do to help your team achieve its goals.

To be there then you need to be here now.

FOLLOW

Another thing you'll learn about leading is that you often don't have to lead. If you study what has to be done and how the people responsible for doing it are doing it, you often find out that there's no need to change what they're doing. In other words, when you're leading skillfully, you're often following.

FLOW

If you learn to lead by learning and following, you'll eventually notice that leadership gravitates naturally to the person most qualified to lead the work on each task that needs to be done. Leadership will flow from person to person in a living current that emerges as if by magic. Leadership is the art of helping the team create and sustain that magical current.

The current of leadership flows with its own peculiar rhythm. Sometimes leaders need to be out in front, showing everyone what to do and how to do it. Sometimes they need to be in the middle, helping, encouraging, and removing obstacles. Sometimes they need to be on the side, watching, listening, and learning. Sometimes they need to be on vacation.

A skillful leader knows when to lead, when to follow, when to talk, when to listen, and when to do nothing at all.

KEEP LEARNING

Sometimes, soon after you find yourself in a situation that requires you to lead, you find out that you don't know enough to do it. You don't know enough about what has to be done, and you don't know enough about the people who have to do it. To be able to lead in a situation like that, you have to know how to learn.

Even when you feel quite confident that you can handle the challenges that leading your team will present, keep learning. You can always get better at what you do.

LEARNING CHANGES BEHAVIOR

Real learning produces significant changes in behavior. You haven't actually acquired new knowledge unless your behavior changes because of it. If your behavior doesn't change significantly after you learn something, what you learned wasn't significant.

To change your behavior, you have to observe it, decide what you want to change, test the change, and practice the changed behavior. That's why I suggest that you test and practice the ideas in this book, and carefully observe and record the results of your tests and your practice.

KNOW YOURSELF

To lead well you have to know yourself – your strengths, your weaknesses, your values, and your blind spots. The next several chapters present exercises that can help you get to know yourself better.

Answer the questions in those chapters in as much detail as you can. Write the answers down in your journal.

If you can't come up with an answer to one of the questions, or your answers don't seem very interesting, BRAINSTORM BY YOURSELF to get more answers.

Just start writing out your thoughts about the question you're trying to answer. Don't censor yourself. If an idea seems crazy or irrelevant, write it down anyway. You may come up with a good idea, but it may appear in language that disguises its relevance to the question you're trying to answer. Be patient. If you keep writing out your thoughts, you'll eventually see where they're leading you. They'll probably take you to some interesting places.

Ask for help from your friends, colleagues, and mentors. Ask them questions. Write down their answers. Here are some questions to ask them:

What do you think are my strengths?
What skills do you think I need to develop to become a better leader?
How do you think I could develop them?
What do you think I could do to improve my ability to communicate with other people?

Think of some more questions to ask. Choose questions that have answers that will help you achieve your goals. Then ask them. Write the answers you get in your journal.

WHOSE LIFE ARE YOU LEADING?

Write answers to the following questions in your journal.

In your opinion, what are the most important things in life?

Why?

How would your parents, teachers, and the other people who have influenced you over the years answer those two questions? Pick a few of those folks and imagine how they would answer those questions. What would they say?

Are your answers the same as theirs?

Why?

Why not?

WHAT DO YOU WANT?

Write answers to the following questions in your journal.

What do you enjoy about your life as it is now?

What don't you enjoy about your life as it is now?

What do you want to do in life that you haven't done yet?

What are you doing now that will enable you to do what you want to do in the future?

What do you want to stop doing?

What are you doing now that will help you stop doing it?

WHAT DO YOU VALUE AND ENJOY?

Write answers to the following questions in your journal. Use brainstorming or some other thinking technique to generate as many detailed answers as you can.

What do you think are the three most valuable things you do?

Why are they valuable?

What are the three most enjoyable things you do?

Why are they enjoyable?

In what ways are the most valuable and most enjoyable things you do different?

How are they the same?

Is there anything about your personality that makes it hard for you to do any of the valuable or enjoyable things you do? Write it down.

Are there any external obstacles that make it hard for you to do any of those things? Write them down.

How could you make it more possible for yourself to do those things?

WHAT OBSTACLES ARE IN YOUR WAY?

Write answers to the following questions in your journal.

Is there anything that you habitually do that you would like to stop doing?

Why do you do it, and why do you want to stop doing it?

What features of your environment make it hard for you to stop doing it?

How could you make it easier for yourself to stop?

SET PRIORITIES

Write answers to the following questions in your journal:

What's the most important task in front of you at this moment?

Why?

Try answering those two questions again, only this time pretend that this is the last year of your life.

Did your answers change?

How?

Try pretending that this is the last day of your life, and answer the questions again.

How did your answers change?

TAKE YOUR TIME

Sometimes you'll find yourself hurrying. Ask yourself why.

Maybe you didn't schedule enough time for the task you're trying to complete. Fix that. Start measuring the time it takes to complete tasks. Then allow that amount of time, and some extra time for overcoming unexpected obstacles, when you schedule those tasks.

Maybe you tried to fit "just one more little task" into a short interval of free time that appeared unexpectedly, and there wasn't enough extra time to do that. Stop doing "just one more little task".

If some unexpected free time comes your way, relax and enjoy it. Look around, find something beautiful to look at or some pleasant music to listen to. Do something relaxing that you can stop as soon as duty calls again.

Maybe you're trying to do two things at once. Don't do that. If you try to do two things at once you'll do neither of them well.

If you find yourself thinking about the next task you have to perform before you've finished the one you're working on, stop, and focus on what you're doing now.

Most of us have been conditioned to dwell on the past or the future instead of focusing on what we're doing in the moment. When you see yourself doing that, return your attention to what you're doing now.

Relax. There's plenty of time to do what you need to do if you don't waste time worrying about the future or dwelling on the past. Thinking about the past or the future is only useful if it helps you do something to improve the future. If it keeps you from doing what you need to do now it's harmful.

BE YOURSELF

You probably know someone who describes himself or herself as: "the kind of person who (fill in the blank)", and then proves by their actions that they aren't that kind of person.

Don't describe yourself. Just be yourself.

To lead well you have to know your teammates – their strengths, their weaknesses, their values, and their blind spots. The next several chapters present exercises that can help you get to know them better. The references for this chapter offer some more tools for doing that..

WORK TO UNDERSTAND YOUR TEAMMATES.

You don't understand a person unless you can predict what they'll do in response to the great majority of the situations that they're likely to encounter.

Often when we think we know the reasons for another person's actions, we're actually imagining that we know. It's hard to step into another person's shoes and see things as they see them. It's hard, but it's worth the effort.

Here's a way to begin:

Try to imagine being that person. What would your daily life be like? What would you want? What problems would you have?

Observe the other person. Do their actions make sense in terms of what you think their daily life is like? In terms of what you think they want? Of the problems you think they face?

While you're observing them, be courteous in your dealings with them, but be careful not to embarrass them by giving them unwanted attention. BUILD TRUST. AVOID EXPRESSING NEGATIVE EMOTIONS. Remember:WE'RE ALL DOING OUR BEST.

If and when they seem to trust you, ask them about their life. What is it like to be them? What do they want? What's keeping them from getting it? If you've earned their trust you probably won't have to ask many questions. They'll just start telling you. Then LISTEN.

If you can do what I suggest, you'll experience a revelation. You'll find out that the person you're trying to understand is different from the person you thought they were. And you'll probably find out that in the most important things, they're not that different from you.

LISTEN

To actually hear what someone else is saying, including their tone of voice, and see their face, their gestures, and their posture – in other words, to get a the best understanding you can of what they're thinking and feeling – you need to be able to silence your own internal monologue. That's not easy. Try to do it for 30 seconds. Now.

What happened? What probably happened is what usually happens to me. The internal monologue doesn't stop, no matter what I'm doing, or not doing, to stop it.

To stop your internal monologue when you're listening to someone else you have to control your attention, focus it on what the other person is saying, how they're saying it, and how they look as they say it. That takes effort. You can't be doing anything else while you're trying to do that.

ASK QUESTIONS.

After they've talked for a while it's a good idea to stop them and try to repeat what they said in your own words. Then check with them to see if they agree that you understood them. If they say you didn't, ask them what you got right and what you got wrong. Then try again. Keep trying until they say you got it all right.

Going back and forth to clarify the meaning of what we're saying to each other can add a lot more precision to our communication. Try it. You'll like it.

ASK QUESTIONS

Ask questions. Gently. Don't assume that you already know the answers.

"What do you plan to do?"

"What do you think is the most important thing to do right now?"

"Why?"

"How do you plan to do it?"

"What possible problems do you anticipate?"

"How do you plan to solve them?"

Practice those questions. At first it may be hard to remember to ask them. Keep practicing.

The references for this chapter, particularly *How to Solve It*, list other useful questions you can ask. If you study them and use the questions they present for a while, you'll get good at helping your teammates and friends come up with solutions to their problems.

WHAT DO THEY WANT?

What do you think your friends and teammates want out of life?

Have you asked them?

Try it. Spend some one-on-one time with each of the people who are important in your life and ask them the questions I've suggested that you ask yourself.

Write down their answers in your journal.

WHAT DO WE WANT?

People who have similar goals usually enjoy working together. They may also be able to help each other. People who don't have similar goals are probably wasting the time they spend together.

What goals do you share with your friends and co-workers?

What goals don't you share with them?

Write descriptions of your shared and differing goals in your journal.

FIND SHARED GOALS

When you lead people you help them, and yourself, achieve goals that you and they share. A goal may be as simple as having food for the next week. It may be as complex as having a successful business.

The most important thing about a goal is your willingness to pursue it. The next most important thing about a goal is whether you share it with the people who are important to you.

Often all you need to do to lead people is to remind them of the goals they're trying to achieve, and ask them what they think they need to do to achieve them.

AGREE ON YOUR GOALS

Work with your teammates to establish general goals. Work until everyone agrees on the goals. Use the consensus-building methods presented in *The Facilitator's Guide to Participatory Decision-Making* and *We the People* - two of the references for this chapter.

If you don't agree on a goal, talk things over. Maybe the statement of the goal needs to be changed for everyone to understand it. Maybe the goal needs to be changed or abandoned.

If you can't agree on your goals, it doesn't make sense to stay together as a team. You need to disband, or some people need to leave and form or join another team.

Some rules for discussing goals:

1. No one talks unless recognized by the discussion leader. You don't have to be the discussion leader. It's often better if you aren't.
2. Don't criticize. There are no good or bad ideas, only ideas that we decide to use, and ideas that we decide not to use. Criticism of ideas, especially when they're first suggested, inhibits people and limits the effectiveness of the discussion.
3. Don't interrupt each other. Try to keep comments and suggestions short.

Use the method I describe in BRAINSTORM WITH YOUR TEAMMATES to record the goals.

Have someone transcribe and distribute the record of the meeting to the team.

DECIDE BY CONSENSUS WHENEVER YOU CAN

People work together much better when they feel that they can influence decisions about what they will do and how they will do it. Consensus decision-making gives everyone on the team maximum influence on such decisions. That approach is far better than letting the official leadership impose decisions on the team.

There are some very effective methods for helping people make decisions by consensus. The references for this section include *The Facilitator's Guide to Participatory Decision-Making* and *We the People* - the two best books I've found that teach those methods. Study them and use the methods they teach.

GET OUT IN FRONT

Don't tell people what to do. Show them.

Model the behavior you think works best. Show the team how you think they can work best by doing your work that way.

BE CONFIDENT, BUT NOT OVERCONFIDENT

Be confident. If a team really wants to do something, it can very likely do it. Well-led, highly-motivated teams have often achieved things that most people thought no one could achieve.

However, even when you know what you're doing and you're doing your best, you don't know enough to predict future events with complete certainty. This is a very complex world, and we know much less about it than there is to know, so it pays to keep your eyes open and guard against overconfidence.

TRUST YOURSELF, BUT NOT ABSOLUTELY

When you start learning how to do something new you may be reluctant to try things. Don't be. A lot of what you try will probably work.

As you gain experience, you'll be surer about the right thing to do in more situations. And when you've gained mastery, you'll be right almost all the time. Almost.

When doubt, ask the people you trust most for advice on what to do. You don't have to take it, but you'll usually want to.

SOMETIMES YOU HAVE TO GO IT ALONE

Sometimes almost everyone you talk to about what you're doing will disagree with you. Maybe everyone will. Alarm bells should go off in your head when that happens.

But you may still be right. That can be a very lonely feeling.

Talk the situation over with the people who disagree with you. Ask them why they disagree. LISTEN to what they say. Restate their points of view in your own words. Ask them if you've stated their points of view correctly. Don't restate your point of view unless they ask you to do that.

See if you can agree with them on the goals you're trying to achieve. Often you'll discover points that you agree on among the points you disagree on. Work through the points you disagree on by asking them more questions.

Sometimes they'll come around to your point of view. If they don't, and you still feel the same after understanding their viewpoint, you may have to go it alone.

BE CAREFUL WHEN YOU MAKE A SPEECH

Only rarely will you have to make a speech. Occasionally you will – when you need to explain and advocate the culture you're trying to establish and maintain, when you need to explain a change in external circumstances that requires a change in the team's goals or to the way the team will work together, when you want to express your respect for your team, and for other reasons that will probably become clear as the team evolves.

When you need to make a speech, remember that it's a special occasion and prepare yourself accordingly. Write the speech out and edit it carefully. Make sure it says exactly what you want it to say.

Imagine that you're the President of the United States, making a speech that all of your political opponents will scrutinize, looking for points to criticize. In a similar way, the people you're leading will all be listening quite attentively, trying to figure out how what you're saying will affect them personally.

You may not have to read the speech when you give it – it's better if you don't – but keep your notes handy, so if you need to you can look at them to remind yourself of what you want to say and how you want to say it.

If you try to do everything perfectly the first time, you won't get much done. It's better to get 80 percent of the job right on the first try and improve the results from there. Sometimes you'll start off in the wrong direction and have to start over, but often just getting moving on a task will show you how to do it.

DO THE EASY THINGS FIRST

A friend once told me that he used to try to do the most difficult tasks in a project first, thinking that would help him avoid problems during the crunch-time at the end of the project. It didn't work.

On the other hand, if you start with the easy tasks, you succeed early and build confidence. That also gives you time to work on improving the way you work together as a team. As the team gets more competent and confident, it can take on the more difficult tasks and succeed.

LEARN FROM MISTAKES

If you think you see a mistake, don't try to fix responsibility for it on one person. The entire team is responsible. You're responsible.

Mistakes are inevitable when you're trying to do new things. It has often been said that if you're not making mistakes, you're not learning.

Right and wrong depend on goals anyway. What's wrong for achieving one goal can be right for achieving another. When you think someone is making a mistake, it may just be that you disagree with him or her about a goal or about how to achieve it.

Take time to find the causes of mistakes without blaming the people who made them. Use one or more of the resources for this chapter to learn how.

WORK ONE-ON-ONE

The more you work with groups of people, the more you'll realize that you can't work with groups of people. You can only work with individuals.

You need to spend time talking one-on-one with everyone on the team. Do it as often as you can. Schedule time with everyone at regular intervals. Drop in on people and chat. Allow plenty of time to talk through any and all of the issues that may come up. Encourage everyone else on the team to do that too.

SERVE

The best leaders are servants. They serve individual team members by helping them do their work and achieve their personal goals. They serve their teams by helping them achieve their goals. They help their teams serve the larger groups that they belong to. The best leaders serve.

HELP EVERYONE LEARN HOW TO DO EVERYTHING

Everyone on the team should know as much as possible about how to do the team's work, including how to lead the team.

Everyone on the team should have an understudy who can do their job when they get sick, are injured, go on vacation, or leave the team. That includes you. Have everyone on the team teach someone else on the team how to do their job.

Get everyone as well trained in their main job and their understudy job as possible. Devote time and resources to getting everyone the best training available in the skills they need.

HELP EVERYONE GET WHAT THEY WANT

If you've gotten to know your team the way I've suggested in earlier chapters, you'll have a good idea of what everyone on the team wants – their goals and their plans for achieving them. Help them as much as you can.

Don't limit yourself to helping them succeed in their careers. Think of other ways to help them. You won't have to devote much time to it. Providing a little advice or encouragement here and there can help a lot.

Suggesting a good training course , a good book, or the name of a good plumber can mean a lot. You might be able to offer some hints on good places to stay or eat on a vacation to a place you've visited.

In other words, be a good friend to your teammates.

STAY AWARE OF WHAT YOU'RE DOING

The hardest part of learning is remembering what you learn, remembering to test it, and remembering to observe the results of your tests. That's because we're hardly ever aware of ourselves or what we're doing. We do almost everything habitually and unconsciously.

That sounds crazy, doesn't it? Test it. Try to be aware of yourself: "I am reading this book. I see the words on the page. I am here, now, reading this book." Try to notice the colors, sounds, and internal sensations that you experience, like small aches and pains, hunger, or thirst. Watch the thoughts drift through your mind.

When you're talking to someone, try to hear the sound of their voice as well as the meaning of their words. Try to see and remember the color of their eyes, the color and style of the clothes they're wearing, the color of their hair, the size and shape of their face and body.

Try to be aware of yourself as you leave your workplace each day. Try to remember how you leave your work area, where you leave your tools or papers. Then, just before you come in the next day, try to remember how you left things the day before.

At the end of a week, review your experience. How many times did you try to be aware of yourself? Do you have clear memories of those times, including memories of how things looked, felt, and sounded? How about smells? Tastes?

If you're honest with yourself, you'll admit that you weren't aware of yourself or of your surroundings much at all during that week. That won't be a comfortable realization. It could, however, be one of the most important realizations you ever have.

REAL CHANGE ISN'T EASY

Changing our behavior is hard for two main reasons.

First, it requires that we go against habits that we've acquired over long periods of time. Those habits are often deeply ingrained. They can even be habits of thought that are simply wrong – truths taken for falsehoods, falsehoods taken for truths.

Second, we almost never see our actual situation. We imagine it, and we imagine ourselves. We think we know ourselves, but we don't often actually observe what we do and compare it with our pictures of ourselves.

Those two truths are often very hard for us to accept. We want to believe that we control our own destinies and can do what we want, when in fact most of the time our habits have control over us. It takes a lot of hard work to free ourselves from that control.

I don't expect you to accept those assertions without argument. But argument will neither confirm nor refute their truth. One or two simple tests can.

Here's a test:

Choose a habit that you'd like to change. It's best if it's a long-standing habit, but that's not essential to the validity of the test. For example: if you don't brush your teeth before going to bed, try to do it for a week. Or if you don't always make your bed after you get up in the morning, try to do that for a week. Observe the results every day. Write your observations down in your journal.

If you're honest with yourself, the first thing you'll observe is that you don't remember to observe. The second thing you'll observe is that when you do observe your attempts to stop the habit, the behavior is usually already under way before you remember to try to stop it.

START CHANGING BY ACCEPTING YOUR SITUATION

It may be hard for you to accept that you're very seldom aware of what you're doing and that you're a creature of habit, You may try to change quickly, or to forget your realization of your situation. That won't help.

Changing your situation will be hard. It will require a lot of work.

All real change is difficult, even when you understand and accept your situation. It's impossible when you don't.

You'll soon realize that changing yourself is nearly impossible without help. Look for mentors and groups who are working on the changes you want to make. You can find them on the Internet or by asking around locally. Check the resources for this chapter for suggestions. Try them out the way I've suggested in HOW TO TEST AND IDEA and TEST PROSPECTIVE TEAMMATES.

DON'T GIVE UP

The going will get tough at times. It may even look like you'll never be able to change what you want to change. Don't believe it. If you don't give up you'll succeed.

Studies have shown that people who are dieting to lose weight, and who don't give up after going off their diets for a meal or two or a day or two, eventually reach their weight loss goals. If they fall down, they just get back up and go back to work on their goals.

It doesn't matter how many times you fall down; what matters is how many times you get up.

REFERENCES BY CHAPTER

This section lists references for each idea in this book under the title of the chapter that presents that idea. Many of the references appear more than once. That's because they provide helpful information on how to use more than one of the ideas.

This section includes at least one reference for nearly every idea in the book. My intent is to give you many choices. Study the references that appeal to you most and ignore the others.

Refer to the ANNOTATED BIBLIOGRAPHY that follows this section for a description of each reference and information about where to find it. They're listed there in alphabetical order by the name of the source.

AGREE ON YOUR GOALS

Buck, John and Sharon Villines. *We the People.*
Doyle, Michael and David Straus. *How to Make Meetings Work.*
Kaner, Sam, et al. *The Facilitator's Guide to Participatory Decision-Making.*

APOLOGIZE, FIX IT, AND MOVE ON

Berne, Eric. *Games People Play.*
Berne, Eric. *What Do You Say After You Say Hello?*
Collin, Rodney. *The Theory of Conscious Harmony.*
Perls, Frederick J. *Gestalt Therapy Verbatim.*

ASK QUESTIONS

Adams, James L. *Conceptual Blockbusting.*
Polya, Giorgi, *How to Solve It.*

AUTOMATE ROUTINE TASKS

Goldratt, Eliyahu and Jeff Cox. *The Goal: A Process of Ongoing Improvement.*
Highsmith, Jim. *Agile Project Management.*

AVOID EXPRESSING NEGATIVE EMOTIONS

Collin, Rodney. *The Theory of Conscious Harmony.*
Covey, Steven J. *The Seven Habits of Highly Effective People.*
Ouspensky, Peter. *The Fourth Way.*
Ouspensky, Peter. *The Psychology of Man's Possible Evolution.*
Vitale, Joe and Hew Len Ph.D. *Zero Limits.*

AVOID HIERARCHIES

Buck, John and Sharon Villines. *We the People.*
Peters, Thomas J. and Robert H. Waterman. *In Search of Excellence.*
Peters, Thomas J. and Nancy K. Austin. *A Passion for Excellence.*
Peters, Thomas J. *Thriving on Chaos.*

AVOID UNNECESSARY MEETINGS

Doyle, Michael and David Straus. *How to Make Meetings Work.*
LeBoeuf, Michael. *Working Smart.*
Weinberg, Gerald M. *Quality Software Management: Volume 2: First Order Measurement.*

AVOID WORKING OVERTIME

LeBoeuf, Michael. *Working Smart.*
Ouspensky, Peter. *The Fourth Way.*
Weinberg, Gerald M. *More Secrets of Consulting.*

BE AT YOUR BEST FOR THE HARDEST TASKS

Covey, Steven R. *The Seven Habits of Highly Effective People.*
Heider, John. *The Tao of Leadership.*
LeBoeuf, Michael. *Working Smart.*
Strozzi-Heckler, Richard. *In Search of the Warrior Spirit.*

BE CAREFUL HOW YOU ECONOMIZE

Weinberg, Gerald M. *Quality Software Management, Volume 1: Systems Thinking.*

BE CAREFUL WHEN YOU MAKE A SPEECH

Carnegie, Dale. *How to Win Friends and Influence People.*
Toastmasters International.

BE CONFIDENT, BUT NOT OVERCONFIDENT

Perls, Frederick J. *Gestalt Therapy Verbatim.*
Perls, Frederick J. *In and Out of the Garbage Pail.*
Rogers, Carl and Barry Stevens. *On Becoming a Person.*
Saitr, Virginia. *Making Contact.*
Satir, Virginia. *The New Peoplemaking.*

BE YOURSELF

Perls, Frederick J. *Gestalt Therapy Verbatim.*
Perls, Frederick J. *In and Out of the Garbage Pail.*
Rogers, Carl and Barry Stevens. *On Becoming a Person.*
Saitr, Virginia. *Making Contact.*
Satir, Virginia. *The New Peoplemaking.*
Zannos, Susan. *Human Types.*

BORN LEADERS, MADE LEADERS, AND FOLLOWERS

Ambrose, Stephen E., *Band of Brothers.*
Covey, Stephen R. *The Seven Habits of Highly Effective People.*
Department of the Army. *FM 22-100 Army Leadership.*
Heider, John. *The Tao of Leadership.*
Strozzi-Heckler, Richard. *In Search of the Warrior Spirit.*
Weinberg, Gerald M. *Becoming a Technical Leader.*
Weinberg, Gerald M. www.ayeconference.com
Weinberg, Gerald M. www.geraldmweinberg.com

BRAINSTORM BY YOURSELF

Adams, James L. *Conceptual Blockbusting.*
De Bono, Edward. *De Bono's Thinking Course.*
Polya, George. *How to Solve It.*

BRAINSTORM WITH YOUR TEAMMATES

Adams, James L. *Conceptual Blockbusting.*
De Bono, Edward. *De Bono's Thinking Course.*
Polya, George. *How to Solve It.*
Kaner, Sam, et al. *The Facilitator's Guide to Participatory Decision-Making.*

BUILD A PERSONAL SUPPORT TEAM

Consumers Union. *Consumer Reports.*
Guillebeau, Chris. http://chrisguillebeau.com/3x5/
LeBoeuf, Michael. *Working Smart.*
www.yelp.com.

BUILD TRUST

Ambrose, Stephen E., *Band of Brothers.*
Berne, Eric. *Games People Play.*
Covey, Stephen R. *The Seven Habits of Highly Effective People.*
Department of the Army. *FM 22-100 Army Leadership.*
Heider, John. *The Tao of Leadership.*
Peters, Thomas J. *Thriving on Chaos.*
Satir, Virginia. *Making Contact.*
Strozzi-Heckler, Richard. *In Search of the Warrior Spirit.*
Weinberg, Gerald M. www.ayeconference.com
Weinberg, Gerald M. *Becoming a Technical Leader.*
Weinberg, Gerald M. www.geraldmweinberg.com
Weinberg, Gerald M. *Quality Software Management, Volume 3: Congruent Action.*

BUILD YOUR TEAM WITH CARE

Holmes, Chet. *The Ultimate Sales Machine.*
Peters, Thomas J. and Robert H. Waterman. *In Search of Excellence.*
Peters, Thomas J. and Nancy K. Austin. *A Passion for Excellence.*
Peters, Thomas J. *Thriving on Chaos.*
Strozzi-Heckler, Richard. *In Search of the Warrior Spirit.*

CHOOSE YOUR TOOLS WITH CARE

Consumers Union. *Consumer Reports.*

DECIDE BY CONSENSUS WHENEVER YOU CAN

Buck, John and Sharon Villines. *We the People.*
Doyle, Michael and David Straus. *How to Make Meetings Work.*
Kaner, Sam, et al. *The Facilitator's Guide to Participatory Decision-Making.*

DO IT NOW

Covey, Stephen R. *The Seven Habits of Highly Effective People.*
LeBoeuf, Michael. *Working Smart.*

DO THE EASY THINGS FIRST

Deming, W. Edwards. *Out of the Crisis.*
Crosby, Philip. *Quality is Free.*
Peters, Thomas J. and Robert H. Waterman. *In Search of Excellence.*
Peters, Thomas J. and Nancy K. Austin. *A Passion for Excellence.*
Peters, Thomas J. *Thriving on Chaos.*
Weinberg, Gerald M. *Quality Software Management, Volume 4: Anticipating Change.*

DO THE LITTLE THINGS WELL

Covey, Stephen R. *The Seven Habits of Highly Effective People.*
LeBoeuf, Michael. *Working Smart.*
Peters, Thomas J., and Robert H. Waterman. *In Search of Excellence.*
Peters, Thomas J. and Nancy K. Austin. *A Passion for Excellence.*
Peters, Thomas J. *Thriving on Chaos.*
Weinberg, Gerald M. *Becoming a Technical Leader.*
Weinberg, Gerald M. www.ayeconference.com

DO WHAT YOU SAY YOU'LL DO

Covey, Stephen R. *The Seven Habits of Highly Effective People.*
Kidder, John Tracy. *The Soul of a New Machine.*
LeBoeuf, Michael. *Working Smart.*
Strozzi-Heckler, Richard. *In Search of the Warrior Spirit.*

DO WHAT YOU WERE MADE TO DO

Anderson, Nancy. *Work with Passion.*
Bowles, Richard. *What Color Is Your Parachute?*
Covey, Stephen R. *The Seven Habits of Highly Effective People.*
Guillebeau, Chris. http://chrisguillebeau.com/3x5/
Needleman, Jacob. *Money and the Meaning of Life.*
Niehardt, Richard. *Black Elk Speaks.*
Sinetar, Marsha. *Do What You Love, and the Money Will Follow.*
Zannos, Susan. *Human Types.*

DON'T FALL IN LOVE WITH PLANNING TOOLS

Weinberg, Gerald M. *Quality Software Management, Volume 1: Systems Thinking.*
Weinberg, Gerald M. *Quality Software Management: Volume 2: First Order Measurement.*
Weinberg, Gerald M. *Quality Software Management, Volume 3: Congruent Action.*

DON'T GET FASCINATED BY TECHNOLOGY

Weinberg, Gerald M. *Quality Software Management, Volume 1: Systems Thinking.*
Weinberg, Gerald M. *Quality Software Management: Volume 2: First Order Measurement.*
Weinberg, Gerald M. *Quality Software Management, Volume 3: Congruent Action.*

DON'T GIVE UP

Collin, Rodney. *The Theory of Conscious Harmony.*
Haven, Girard. *Creating a Soul.*
Kapleau, Philip. *The Three Pillars of Zen.*
Ouspensky, Peter. *In Search of the Miraculous.*
Ouspensky, Peter. *The Psychology of Man's Possible Evolution.*
Tolle, Eckhart. *The Power of Now.*

DON'T HOLD GRUDGES

Berne, Eric. *Games People Play.*
Collin, Rodney. *The Theory of Conscious Harmony.*
Covey, Steven J. *The Seven Habits of Highly Effective People.*
Ouspensky, Peter. *The Fourth Way.*

DON'T MAKE EXCUSES

Ambrose, Stephen E. *Band of Brothers.*
Covey, Stephen R. *The Seven Habits of Highly Effective People.*
LeBoeuf, Michael. *Working Smart.*
Strozzi-Heckler, Richard. *In Search of the Warrior Spirit.*

DON'T REACT - RESPOND

Haven, Girard. *Creating a Soul.*
Ouspensky, Peter. *The Fourth Way.*
Ouspensky, Peter. *The Psychology of Man's Possible Evolution.*
Weinberg, Gerald M., *Quality Software Management, Volume 3: Congruent Action.*
Vitale, Joe and Hew Len Ph. D. *Zero Limits.*

DON'T SUGGEST SOLUTIONS

Adams, James L. *Conceptual Blockbusting.*
Blanchard, Kenneth. *The One-Minute Manager.*
De Bono, Edward. *De Bono's Thinking Course.*
Kaner, Sam, et al. *The Facilitator's Guide to Participatory Decision-Making.*
Polya, George. *How to Solve It.*

DON'T TELL - ASK

Blanchard, Kenneth. *The One-Minute Manager.*
Heider, John. *The Tao of Leadership.*
Weinberg, Gerald M. *Becoming a Technical Leader.*
Weinberg, Gerald M. *More Secrets of Consulting.*
Weinberg, Gerald M. *Quality Software Management: Volume 3: Congruent Action.*
Weinberg, Gerald M. *The Secrets of Consulting.*
Weinberg, Gerald M. www.ayeconference.com

EFFECTIVE TEAMS ARE PRECIOUS

Peters, Thomas J. and Robert H. Waterman. *In Search of Excellence.*
Peters, Thomas J. and Nancy K. Austin. *A Passion for Excellence.*
Peters, Thomas J. *Thriving on Chaos.*

FIND MENTORS

Anderson, Nancy. *Work with Passion.*
Weinberg, Gerarld M. *The Secrets of Consulting.*
Weinberg, Gerald M. *More Secrets of Consulting.*
Bowles, Richard. *What Color is Your Parachute?*

FIND SHARED GOALS

Buck, John and Sharon Villines. *We the People.*
Kaner, Sam, et al. *The Facilitators Guide to Participatory Decision-Making.*
Perls, Frederick J. *Gestalt Therapy Verbatim.*
Perls, Frederick J. *In and Out of the Garbage Pail.*
Rogers, Carl. *On Becoming a Person.*
Saitr, Virginia. *Making Contact.*
Satir, Virginia. *The New Peoplemaking.*

FLOW

Heider, John. *The Tao of Leadership.*

FOLLOW

Heider, John. *The Tao of Leadership.*

GET A LOT OF FACE TIME

Perls, Frederick J. *Gestalt Therapy Verbatim.*
Peters, Thomas J. and Nancy K. Austin. *A Passion for Excellence.*
Rogers, Carl and Barry Stevens. *On Becoming a Person.*
Satir, Virgina. *Making Contact.*

GET HELP

Burton, Robert Earl. *Self-Remembering.*
Collin, Rodney. *The Theory of Conscious Harmony.*
Haven, Girard. *Creating a Soul.*
Kapleau, Philip. *The Three Pillars of Zen.*
Ouspensky, Peter. *In Search of the Miraculous.*
Ouspensky, Peter. *The Psychology of Man's Possible Evolution.*
www.livingpresence.com

GET HELP LEARNING ABOUT YOURSELF

Rogers, Carl and Barry Stevens. *On Becoming a Person.*
Saitr, Virginia. *Making Contact.*
Satir, Virginia. *The New Peoplemaking.*
Zannos, Susan. *Human Types.*

GET OUT IN FRONT

Ambrose, Stephen E. *Band of Brothers.*
Heider, John. *The Tao of Leadership.*

GET THE BEST TOOLS YOU CAN AFFORD

Consumers Union. *Consumer Reports.*

GET UNSTUCK

Adams, James L. *Conceptual Blockbusting.*
De Bono, Edward. *De Bono's Thinking Course.*
Polya, George. *How to Solve It.*

GIVE FEEDBACK

Blanchard, Kenneth, et al. *The One-Minute Manager.*
Satir, Virginia. *Making Contact.*
Satir, Virginia. *The New Peoplemaking.*
Strozzi-Heckler, Richard. *In Search of the Warrior Spirit.*

HAVE FUN

Berne, Eric. *Games People Play.*
Berne, Eric. *What Do You Say After You Say Hello?*
Peters, Thomas J. *Thriving on Chaos.*
Strozzi-Heckler, Richard. *In Search of the Warrior Spirit.*

HELP EVERYONE GET WHAT THEY WANT

Bowles, Richard. *What Color Is Your Parachute?*
Satir, Virginia. *The New Peoplemaking.*

HELP EVERYONE LEARN HOW TO DO EVERYTHING

Peters, Thomas J. *Thriving on Chaos.*
Weinberg, Gerald M. *Becoming a Technical Leader.*
Weinberg, Gerald M. *Quality Software Management: Volume 4: Anticipating Change.*

HOW TO TEST AN IDEA

De Bono, Edward. *De Bono's Thinking Course.*
Feynman, Richard. *Surely You're Joking, Mr. Feynman!*
Polya, George *How to Solve It.*
Weinberg, Gerald M. *An Introduction to General Systems Thinking.*

IGNORE USELESS IDEAS

De Bono, Edward. *De Bono's Thinking Course.*
Polya, George. *How to Solve It.*
Shah, Idries. *Learning How to Learn.*
Weinberg, Gerald M. *The Secrets of Consulting.*

INVEST IN PROCESS IMPROVEMENT

Crosby, Philip. *Quality is Free.*
Deming, W. Edwards. *Out of the Crisis.*
Goldratt, Eliyahu and Jeff Cox. *The Goal: A Process of Ongoing Improvement.*
Highsmith, Jim. *Agile Project Management.*
Peters, Thomas J. and Robert H. Waterman. *In Search of Excellence.*
Peters, Thomas J. and Nancy K. Austin. *A Passion for Excellence.*
Peters, Thomas J. *Thriving on Chaos.*

IT'S NOT ABOUT BEING A NICE GUY

Ambrose, Stephen E. *Band of Brothers.*
Berne, Eric. *Games People Play.*
Berne, Eric. *The Structure and Dynamics of Organizations and Groups.*
Covey, Stephen R. *The Seven Habits of Highly Effective People.*
Department of the Army. *FM 22-100 Army Leadership.*
Heider, John. *The Tao of Leadership.*
Peters, Thomas J. *Thriving on Chaos.*
Satir, Virginia. *Making Contact.*
Strozzi-Heckler, Richard. *In Search of the Warrior Spirit.*
Weinberg, Gerald M. www.ayeconference.com
Weinberg, Gerald M. *Becoming a Technical Leader.*
Weinberg, Gerald M. www.geraldmweinberg.com
Weinberg, Gerald M. *Quality Software Management, Volume 3: Congruent Action.*

KEEP A JOURNAL

Conner, Janet. *Writing Down Your Soul.*
Grason, Sandy. *Journalution.*

KEEP EVERYONE INFORMED

Heider, John. *The Tao of Leadership.*
Peters, Thomas J. *Thriving on Chaos.*

KEEP IMPROVING THE WAYS YOU DO THINGS

Crosby, Philip. *Quality is Free.*
Peters, Thomas. *In Search of Excellence.*
Peters, Thomas. *A Passion for Excellence.*
Peters, Thomas. *Thriving on Chaos.*
Weinberg, Gerald M. *Quality Software Management, Volume 4: Anticipating Change.*

KEEP LEARNING

Heider, John. *The Tao of Leadership.*
Perls, Frederic. *Gestalt Therapy Verbatim.*
Satir, Virginia. *The New Peoplemaking.*
Shah, Idries. *Learning How to Learn.*

KEEP YOUR PROMISES TO YOURSELF

Covey, Stephen R. *The Seven Habits of Highly Effective People.*
LeBoeuf, Michael. *Working Smart.*
Strozzi-Heckler, Richard. *In Search of the Warrior Spirit.*
Weinberg, Gerald M. *The Secrets of Consulting.*

KNOW HOW

Weinberg, Gerald M. *Becoming a Technical Leader.*
Weinberg, Gerald M. *Quality Software Management: Volume 1: Systems Thinking.*

KNOW YOUR TEAMMATES

Perls, Frederick J. *Gestalt Therapy Verbatim.*
Perls, Frederick J. *In and Out of the Garbage Pail.*
Rogers, Carl. *On Becoming a Person.*
Saitr, Virginia. *Making Contact.*
Satir, Virginia. *The New Peoplemaking.*
Zannos, Susan. *Human Types.*

KNOW YOURSELF

Bowles, Richard. *What Color is Your Parachute?*
Zannos, Susan. *Human Types.*

LEAD NOW

Burton, Robert Earl. *Self-Remembering.*
Heider, John. *The Tao of Leadership.*
Kapleau, Philip. *The Three Pillars of Zen.*
Ram Dass. *Be Here Now.*
Tolle, Eckhart. *The Power of Now.*

LEARN FROM MISTAKES

Heider, John. *The Tao of Leadership.*
Peters, Thomas J. *Thriving on Chaos.*

LEARNING CHANGES BEHAVIOR

Heider, John. *The Tao of Leadership.*
Perls, Frederic. *Gestalt Therapy Verbatim.*
Satir, Virginia. *The New Peoplemaking.*
Shah, Idries. *Learning How to Learn.*

LEAVE THE DETAILS UNTIL THE END

Peters, Thomas J. and Robert H. Waterman. *In Search of Excellence.*
Peters, Thomas J. and Nancy K. Austin. *A Passion for Excellence.*
Peters, Thomas J. *Thriving on Chaos.*
Weinberg, Gerald M. *Quality Software Management, Volume 4: Anticipating Change.*

LISTEN

Perls, Frederick J. *Gestalt Therapy Verbatim.*
Perls, Frederick J. *In and Out of the Garbage Pail.*
Rogers, Carl and Barry Stevens. *On Becoming a Person.*
Saitr, Virginia. *Making Contact.*

MEASURE

Crosby, Philip. *Quality is Free.*
Deming, W. Edwards. *Out of the Crisis.*
Weinberg, Gerald M. *Quality Software Management: Volume 2, First Order Measurement.*

MEASURE IMROVEMENT

Crosby, Philip. *Quality is Free.*
Deming, W. Edwards. *Out of the Crisis.*
Peters, Thomas J. and Robert H. Waterman. *In Search of Excellence.*
Peters, Thomas J. and Nancy K. Austin. *A Passion for Excellence.*
Peters, Thomas J. *Thriving on Chaos.*
Weinberg, Gerald M. *Quality Software Management, Volume 1: Systems Thinking.*
Weinberg, Gerald M. *Quality Software Management, Volume 2: First Order Measurement*
.

MIX IT UP

LeBoeuf, Michael. *Working Smart.*
Ouspensky, Peter. *The Fourth Way.*
Weinberg, Gerald M. *More Secrets of Consulting.*

OTHER SOURCES OF IDEAS

Adams, James L. *Conceptual Blockbusting.*
Bowles, Richard. *What Color Is Your Parachute?*
LeBoeuf, Michael. *Working Smart.*

PIGHEADED DISCIPLINE AND DETERMINATION

Holmes, Chet. *The Ultimate Sales Machine.*
LeBoeuf, Michael. *Working Smart.*
Peters, Thomas J., and Robert H. Waterman. *In Search of Excellence.*
Peters, Thomas J. and Nancy K. Austin. *A Passion for Excellence.*
Peters, Thomas J. *Thriving on Chaos.*
Weinberg, Gerald M. *The Secrets of Consulting.*

PLAN BACKWARD

McConnell, Steve. *Rapid Development.*
Weinberg, Gerald M. *Quality Software Management: Volume 1: Systems Thinking.*
Weinberg, Gerald M. *Quality Software Management: Volume 2: First Order Measurement.*

POINT OUT WHAT NEEDS TO IMPROVE

Crosby, Philip. *Quality is Free.*
Peters, Thomas. *In Search of Excellence.*
Peters, Thomas. *A Passion for Excellence.*
Peters, Thomas. *Thriving on Chaos.*
Weinberg, Gerald M. *Quality Software Management, Volume 1: Systems Thinking.*
Weinberg, Gerald M. *Quality Software Management, Volume 2: First Order Measurement.*

PRACTICE USING IDEAS THAT YOU FIND USEFUL

Aikido
Weinberg, Gerald M. *The Secrets of Consulting.*

REAL CHANGE ISN'T EASY

Collin, Rodney. *The Theory of Conscious Harmony.*
Kapleau, Philip. *The Three Pillars of Zen.*
Ouspensky, Peter. *In Search of the Miraculous.*
Ouspensky, Peter. *The Psychology of Man's Possible Evolution.*

RESPECT EVERYONE

Collin, Rodney. *The Theory of Conscious Harmony.*
Perls, Frederick J. *Gestalt Therapy Verbatim.*
Rogers, Carl and Barry Stevens. *On Becoming a Person.*
Satir, Virginia. *The New Peoplemaking.*

SAY GOODBY KINDLY

Berne, Eric. *Games People Play.*
Berne, Eric. *The Structure and Dynamics of Organizations and Groups.*
Rogers, Carl and Barry Stevens. *On Becoming a Person.*
Satir, Virginia. *Making Contact.*
Weinberg, Gerald M. *Quality Software Management, Volume 3: Congruent Action.*

SERVE

Collin, Rodney. *The Theory of Conscious Harmony.*
Heider, John. *The Tao of Leadership.*
Kapleau, Philip. *The Three Pillars of Zen.*

SET PRIORITIES

Bowles, Richard. *What Color Is Your Parachute?*
Covey, Stephen R. *The Seven Habits of Highly Effective People.*
Heider, John. *The Tao of Leadership.*

SMALL IS BEAUTIFUL

Ambrose, Stephen E., *Band of Brothers.*
Heider, John. *The Tao of Leadership.*
Peters, Thomas J. *Thriving on Chaos.*
Schumacher, E.F. *Small Is Beautiful.*
Strozzi-Heckler, Richard. *In Search of the Warrior Spirit.*

SOME LARGE ORGANIZATIONS WORK

Buck, John and Sharon Villines. *We the People.*
Peters, Thomas J. and Robert H. Waterman. *In Search of Excellence.*
Peters, Thomas J. and Nancy K. Austin. *A Passion for Excellence.*
Peters, Thomas J. *Thriving on Chaos.*

SOME THINGS WILL HAVE TO GO

Berne. Eric. *Games People Play.*
Kapleau, Philip. *The Three Pillars of Zen.*
LeBoeuf, Michael. *Working Smart.*
Perls, Frederick J. *Gestalt Therapy Verbatim.*
Perls, Frederick J. *In and Out of the Garbage Pail.*
Rogers, Carl, and Barry Stevens. *Person to Person.*
Satir, Virginia. *The New People-Making.*
Weinberg, Gerald M. *The Secrets of Consulting.*

SOMETIMES YOU HAVE TO GO IT ALONE

Ambrose, Stephen E. *Band of Brothers.*
Perls, Frederick J. *Gestalt Therapy Verbatim.*
Perls, Frederick J. *In and Out of the Garbage Pail.*
Rogers, Carl and Barry Stevens. *On Becoming a Person.*
Saitr, Virginia. *Making Contact.*
Satir, Virginia. *The New Peoplemaking.*

SPEND YOUR TIME WISELY

Covey, Steven R. *The Seven Habits of Highly Effective People.*
LeBoeuf, Michael. *Working Smart.*

START CHANGING BY ACCEPTING YOUR SITUATION

Collin, Rodney. *The Theory of Conscious Harmony.*
Haven, Girard. *Creating a Soul.*
Kapleau, Philip. *The Three Pillars of Zen.*
Ouspensky, Peter. *In Search of the Miraculous.*
Ouspensky, Peter. *The Psychology of Man's Possible Evolution.*
Tolle, Eckhart. *The Power of Now.*

STAY AWARE OF WHAT YOU'RE DOING

Collin, Rodney. *The Theory of Conscious Harmony.*
Kapleau, Philip. *The Three Pillars of Zen.*
Ouspensky, Peter. *In Search of the Miraculous.*
Ouspensky, Peter. *The Psychology of Man's Possible Evolution.*

STAY FOCUSED

Kidder, John Tracy. *The Soul of a New Machine.*
LeBoeuf, Michael. *Working Smart.*
Peters, Thomas J.. *Thriving on Chaos.*

STAY OUT OF THE WAY

Blanchard, Kenneth. *The One-Minute Manager.*
Heider, John. *The Tao of Leadership.*
Kaner, Sam, et al. *The Facilitator's Guide to Participatory Decision-Making.*

STAY POSITIVE

Ouspensky, Peter. *The Fourth Way.*
Collin, Rodney. *The Theory of Conscious Harmony.*
Stevens, Barry. *Don't Push the River, It Flows by Itself.*
Niehardt, Richard. *Black Elk Speaks.*

TAKE BREAKS

LeBoeuf, Michael. *Working Smart.*
Ouspensky, Peter. *The Fourth Way.*
Weinberg, Gerald M. *More Secrets of Consulting.*

TAKE CARE OF YOURSELF

Aikido
Berne, Eric. *Games People Play.*
Cohen, Ken. *The Way of Qigong.*
Qigong
Ray, Kali. *In the Flow with Kali Ray.*
Rogers, Carl, and Barry Stevens. *Person to Person.*
Satir, Virginia. *The New People-Making.*
Tai Chi
Ueshiba, Morihei. *The Essence of Aikido.*
Yoga

TAKE TIME OFF

LeBoeuf, Michael. *Working Smart.*
Ouspensky, Peter. *The Fourth Way.*
Weinberg, Gerald M. *More Secrets of Consulting.*
Weinberg, Gerald M. *The Secrets of Consulting.*

TAKE YOUR TIME

Heider, John. *The Tao of Leadership.*
Kapleau, Philip. *The Three Pillars of Zen.*
Ram Dass. *Be Here Now.*
Tolle, Eckhart. The Power of Now.

TELL THE TRUTH

Berne, Eric. *Games People Play.*
Collin, Rodney. *The Theory of Conscious Harmony.*
Perls, Frederick J. *Gestalt Therapy Verbatim.*
Weinberg, Gerald M. *Quality Software Management, Volume 3: Congruent Action.*

TEST NEW IDEAS

De Bono, Edward. *De Bono's Thinking Course.*
Polya, Georgy. *How to Solve It.*
Weinberg, Gerald M. *An Introduction to General Systems Thinking.*

TEST PROSPECTIVE TEAMMATES

Berne, Eric. *Games People Play.*
Berne, Eric. *The Structure and Dynamics of Organizations and Groups.*
Kidder, John Tracy. *The Soul of a New Machine.*
Perls, Frederick J. *Gestalt Therapy Verbatim.*
Rogers, Carl and Barry Stevens. *On Becoming a Person.*
Strozzi-Heckler, Richard. *In Search of the Warrior Spirit.*

THE BEST LEADERS

Ambrose, Stephen E. *Band of Brothers.*
Covey, Stephen R. *The Seven Habits of Highly Effective People.*
Department of the Army. *FM 22-100 Army Leadership.*
Heider, John. *The Tao of Leadership.*
Peters, Thomas J. *Thriving on Chaos.*
Strozzi-Heckler, Richard. *In Search of the Warrior Spirit.*
Weinberg, Gerald M. *Becoming a Technical Leader.*
Weinberg, Gerald M. www.geraldmweinberg.com
Weinberg, Gerald M. www.ayeconference.com
Weinberg, Gerald M. *Quality Software Management, Volume 3: Congruent Action.*

THERE'S NO SILVER BULLET

Weinberg, Gerald M. *Quality Software Management, Volume 1: Systems Thinking.*
Weinberg, Gerald M. *Quality Software Management: Volume 2: First Order Measurement.*
Weinberg, Gerald M. *Quality Software Management, Volume 3: Congruent Action.*

TRUST YOURSELF, BUT NOT ABSOLUTELY

Perls, Frederick J. *Gestalt Therapy Verbatim.*
Perls, Frederick J. *In and Out of the Garbage Pail.*
Rogers, Carl and Barry Stevens. *On Becoming a Person.*
Saitr, Virginia. *Making Contact.*
Satir, Virginia. *The New Peoplemaking.*

USE THE RIGHT TOOLS FOR THE JOB

Weinberg, Gerald M. *Quality Software Management: Volume 1: Systems Thinking.*
Weinberg, Gerald M. *Quality Software Management: Volume 2: First Order Measurement.*

WE'RE ALL DOING OUR BEST

Colllin, Rodney. *The Theory of Celestial Influence.*
Heider, Richard. *The Tao of Leadership.*
Satir, Virginia. *The New Peoplemaking.*
Weinberg, Gerald M. *The Secrets of Consulting.*
Weinberg, Gerald M. *Quality Software Management, Volume 3: Congruent Action.*

WHAT DO THEY WANT?

Perls, Frederick J. *Gestalt Therapy Verbatim.*
Perls, Frederick J. *In and Out of the Garbage Pail.*
Rogers, Carl and Barry Stevens. *On Becoming a Person.*
Saitr, Virginia. *Making Contact.*
Satir, Virginia. *The New Peoplemaking.*

WHAT DO WE WANT?

Buck, John and Sharon Villines. *We the People.*
Kaner, Sam, et al. *The Facilitator's Guide to Participatory Decision-Making.*
Rogers, Carl and Barry Stevens. *On Becoming a Person.*
Saitr, Virginia. *Making Contact.*
Satir, Virginia. *The New Peoplemaking.*

WHAT DO YOU VALUE AND ENJOY?

Bowles, Richard. *What Color Is Your Parachute?*
Rogers, Carl and Barry Stevens. *On Becoming a Person.*
Zannos, Susan. *Human Types.*

WHAT DO YOU WANT?

Bowles, Richard. *What Color is Your Parachute?*
Rogers, Carl and Barry Stevens. *On Becoming a Person.*

WHAT OBSTACLES ARE IN YOUR WAY?

Bowles, Richard. *What Color Is Your Parachute?*
Rogers, Carl and Barry Stevens. *On Becoming a Person.*

WHOSE LIFE ARE YOU LEADING?

Rogers, Carl and Barry Stevens. *On Becoming a Person.*
Satir, Virginia. *The New Peoplemaking.*

WHY LEAD?

Ambrose, Stephen E., *Band of Brothers.*
Department of the Army. *FM 22-100 Army Leadership* .
Heider, John. *The Tao of Leadership.*
Strozzi-Heckler, Richard. *In Search of the Warrior Spirit.*
Weinberg, Gerald M. *Becoming a Technical Leader.*
Weinberg, Gerald M. www.geraldmweinberg.com
Weinberg, Gerald M. www.ayeconference.com

WORK ONE-ON-ONE

Perls, Frederick J. *Gestalt Therapy Verbatim.*
Rogers, Carl and Barry Stevens. *On Becoming a Person.*
Satir, Virgina. *Making Contact.*

WORK TO UNDERSTAND YOUR TEAMMATES

Perls, Frederick J. *Gestalt Therapy Verbatim.*
Perls, Frederick J. *In and Out of the Garbage Pail.*
Rogers, Carl and Barry Stevens. *On Becoming a Person.*
Saitr, Virginia. *Making Contact.*
Satir, Virginia. *The New Peoplemaking.*

YOU MAY ALREADY BE A LEADER

Ambrose, Stephen E., *Band of Brothers.*
Covey, Stephen R. *The Seven Habits of Highly Effective People.*
Department of the Army. *FM 22-100 Army Leadership.*
Heider, John. *The Tao of Leadership.*
Strozzi-Heckler, Richard. *In Search of the Warrior Spirit.*
Weinberg, Gerald M. *Becoming a Technical Leader.*
Weinberg, Gerald M. www.ayeconference.com
Weinberg, Gerald M. www.geraldmweinberg.com

ANNOTATED BIBLIOIGRAPHY

This section contains detailed bibliographical information on all the references for all the ideas this book presents, and tells you how to find them. I've added comments to each entry to give you an idea of what you'll find.

Almost every book listed here can be bought online. Just run an Internet search on the title. The results will probably include links to several sellers. Don't ignore your local library though. There's no reason to buy a book that you may only read once, and may not even finish. If a reference can't be found on the Internet, I tell you how to find it in my comments.

Adams, James L. *Conceptual Blockbusting: a Guide to Better Ideas.* Cambridge, Massachusetts. Perseus Publishing, 2001. This book contains a wealth of information about how we think, and how to do it better. It's full of suggestions for ways to generate new ideas, including a presentation of the brainstorming technique I present in this book. Highly recommended.

Aikido. Aikido is the ultimate martial art – gentle and wonderfully effective. Don't embark on a study of aikido unless you're prepared to persist for a long time. Mastery takes long study, but rewards the persistent student with complete freedom from fear of attack. These days there are aikido masters living in most major cities in the United States. Look for one near you on the Internet. Just search for "Aikido" in your local area - for example, search for "Aikido Atlanta" if you live in Atlanta. Evaluate the people you find the way I suggest in BUILD A PERSONAL SUPPORT NETWORK and CHOOSE YOUR TOOLS WITH CARE. Your first teacher doesn't even have to be a master. If you study long enough, a master will find you.

Ambrose, Stephen E., *Band of Brothers.* New York: Simon and Schuster, 2001.The epic account of the formation and subsequent adventures of what was probably one of the greatest fighting units in the history of warfare. A great adventure story and an example of what a well-led team can do.

Anderson, Nancy. *Work with Passion: How to Do What You Love for a Living*. Novato, California: New World Library, 2004. The title says it all.

Doyle, Michael and David Straus. *How to Make Meetings Work*. New York: Berkeley Books, 1993. Follow the meeting procedure presented in this book and watch the productivity of your team's meetings soar. You'll have many fewer meetings, and get much more done at them.

Berne, Eric. *Games People Play: the Psychology of Human Relations*. New York. Grove Press, 1996. This book is an encyclopedia of the ways people avoid actually making contact with each other. Get the latest edition. It contains useful new material written by Dr. Berne's students after his death. When you find it hard to understand someone's behavior, refer to this book. They're probably playing one of the games it describes.

Berne, Eric. *The Structure and Dynamics of Organizations and Groups*. New York: Random House, 1979. This book explains a lot of what you see when human beings gather in large groups – either organized or not. As insightful as *Games People Play*.

Berne, Eric. *What Do You Say After You Say Hello?* New York: Bantam Books, 1973. This book presents Dr. Berne's understanding of why people talk to each other at all. It's incomplete, but more complete than is common. See the entries for Rodney Collin and Peter Ouspensky for presentations of a more complete understanding of this theme.

Blanchard, Kenneth, and Spencer Johnson, M.D. *The One-Minute Manager*. New York: Harper Collins, 1982. A simplified approach to leadership that nonetheless contains some real wisdom: set clear objectives; praise progress toward them; correct deviations from the right path; do all three as soon as possible; and do all three with as little energy as possible. Good advice. Hard to follow.

Bowles, Richard. *What Color is Your Parachute? A Practical Manual for Job-Hunters and Career-Changers*. New York: Ten Speed Press, published annually. Get the latest edition for access to the most current reference material. This is a wonderful book that I've used and recommended many times. It contains very practical advice on finding and getting exactly the kind of work you want. Richard Bowles is a national treasure. The official website for the book, and for Richard Bowles, is www.jobhuntersbible.com.

Buck, John and Sharon Villines. *We the People: Consenting to a Deeper Democracy.* Washington, D.C.: 2007. This book describes a method of governance - called sociocracy - which is based on what the authors call the principle of consent. The book includes detailed instructions for implementing the method. The authors claim that the method has been very successful in relatively large organizations in Europe and the United States.

Burton, Robert Earl. *Self-Remembering.* York Beach, Maine: Samuel Weizer, 1995. The definitive work on how to be present to the moment in the now. Clearly surpasses Eckart Tolle's *The Power of Now.*

Carnegie, Dale. *How to Win Friends and Influence People.* New York: Simon and Schuster, 1981. This is the classic on how to do just what the title says. If you take the Carnegie course you'll become an excellent public speaker. See also Toastmasters.

Cohen, Kenneth. *The Way of Qigong: The Art and Science of Chinese Energy Healing*. New York: Ballantine Books, 1997. Any edition will do. This is the definitive book in English on Qigong. You can begin your Qigong practice by choosing a daily program from the exercises that Ken describes in it. At some point you'll need a teacher. Look for one on the Internet by searching for "Qigong" in your local area - for example, search for "Qigong Detroit" if you live in Detroit. Then evaluate the people you find the way I suggest in BUILD A PERSONAL SUPPORT NETWORK and CHOOSE YOUR TOOLS WITH CARE.

Collin, Rodney. *The Theory of Celestial Influence.* Boston: Shambala Publications, 1984. Before he died, Peter Ouspensky gave Rodney Collin the task of reconciling the esoteric knowledge he had learned from Mr. Ouspensky with current scientific and historical knowledge. This book is the result of the effort that Mr. Collin made to complete that task. Amazing.

Collin, Rodney. *The Theory of Conscious Harmony.* Sacramento, California: By the Way Books, 1998. This is a posthumously published collection of excerpts from the letters of Rodney Collin, a student of Peter Ouspensky and leader of a group of Fourth Way students centered in Mexico. The excerpts show a deep understanding of human nature and the compassion that such an understanding evokes.

Conner, Janet. *Writing Down Your Soul: How to Activate and Listen to the Extraordinary Voice Within.* San Francisco: Conari Press, 2008. Good ideas on how to keep a journal. A bit flamboyant, but practical. Use your own judgment, but use the advice too.

Consumers Union. *Consumer Reports.* www.consumersunion.org. These folks invented a very effective method of product evaluation. If you imitate them when you're evaluating products and services, you'll probably find the ones best suited to your needs.

Covey, Stephen R. *The Seven Habits of Highly Effective People.* New York: Fireside, 1990. This is, of course, the classic on how to make sure you take care of what's most important to you. Any edition will do, and you can get inexpensive used copies on the Internet. Enjoy.

Crosby, Philip. *Quality is Free.* New York: McGraw-Hill 1979. The definitive argument in favor of the proposition that in the long run it's much less expensive to produce high quality goods and services than it is to cut corners. Highly recommended.

De Bono, Edward. *De Bono's Thinking Course.* New York: Facts on File, 1985. De Bono is a well-known student of human problem-solving behavior, and a creator of training designed to help people become more successful at solving problems. His course is well worth a look. But... don't expect to improve your problem-solving skills without doing a lot of work.

Deming, W. Edwards. *Out of the Crisis.* Cambridge, Massachusetts: MIT Press, 1981. The classic text on how to apply statistical methods to process improvement: Test, Measure, Change, Repeat (forever). Highly recommended.

Department of the Army. *FM 22-100 Army Leadership: Be, Know, Do.* Washington, DC: Headquarters, Department of the Army, 1999. You can download the entire manual from the Internet. It's worth it. The U.S. Army is supposed to be the best in the world. One reason may be that the Army teaches leadership from this manual. It's quite a read.

Feynman, Richard. *Surely You're Joking Mr. Feynman!: Adventures of a Curious Character, with contributions by Ralph Leighton.* New York: W.W. Norton and Company, 1985. Richard Feynman was the personification of "thinking outside the box". Study his approach if you want to learn how to come up with creative solutions to hard problems. Look him up on Wikipedia and YouTube and study some of the audio and video records of his teaching. Really fun. And really smart.

Goldratt, Eliyahu and Jeff Cox. *The Goal: A Process of Ongoing Improvement.* Great Barrington, Massachusetts: North River Press, 2004. A novel about how to analyze business processes. It dramatizes the key constraint method developed by Dr. Goldratt. The method is quite effective. The inventors of the agile software development method used Dr. Goldratt's method to analyze the software development process. The agile software development method was the product of that analysis.

Grason, Sandy. *Journalution: Journaling to Awaken Your Inner Voice, Heal Your Life, and Manifest Your Dreams*. Novato, California: New World Library, 2005. What the title says, even if a little over the top.

Guillebeau, Chris. http://chrisguillebeau.com/3x5/ I find this blog interesting. Chris is full of ideas about how to live the way you want and survive in good style. I especially recommend his free e-book, 279 Days to Overnight Success - a handbook for aspiring bloggers and e-book publishers. If you have dreams of writing and publishing on the Internet, this is the book for you. Browse the site. There's much of interest there.

Haven, Girard. *Creating a Soul.* Oregon House, California: Ulysses Books: 1999. This book shows you how one person has worked for over 35 years to free himself from his most pernicious habits. You should be so lucky – and so persistent .

Heider, John. *The Tao of Leadership: Lao Tzu's Tao Te Ching Adapted for a New Age*. Lake Worth, Florida: Humanics Publishing Group, 1986. When you've finished with this book, study John's book to get to the next level. If you can do what John says Lao Tzu tells leaders to do, you're there.

Highsmith, Jim. *Agile Project Management*. Boston: Addison-Wesley, 2009. This book explains the agile development method, a recently-invented method for developing new products based on the ideas of Dr. Eliyahu Goldratt (referenced above.) The agile method has proven to be a very effective way to develop new products with minimum wasted motion.

Holmes, Chet. *The Ultimate Sales Machine: Turbocharge Your Business with Relentless Focus on 12 Key Strategies*. New York: Penguin Group, 2007. If you can do even half of what Chet tells you to do, you'll be extremely successful at whatever you try. Get it. Read it. Do it.

Kapleau, Philip. *The Three Pillars of Zen*. New York: Doubleday, 1965. If you want to "understand" Zen Buddhism - at least one Japanese version of it - read this book. You can't really understand Zen Buddhism unless you practice it, but this book will get you about as close to a true understanding as you can get without doing that. Highly recommended.

Kaner, Sam, Doyle, Michael, Lind, Lenny, and Catherine Toldi. *The Facilitator's Guide to Participatory Decision-Making*. New York: John Wiley and Sons, 2007. One of the two best books on facilitating the group decision-making process that I've found in over 40 years of looking. The other one is *We the People,* by John Buck and Sharon Villines.

Kidder, John Tracy. *The Soul of a New Machine*. New York: Little Brown, 1981. Tracy Kidder tells the story behind the creation of a new computer – from scratch – by a dedicated team. The crux of the story is the willingness of every member of the team to dedicate himself or herself to completion of each task they had signed up to do. They definitely did what they said they would do – with a vengeance.

LeBoeuf, Michael. *Working Smart: How to Accomplish More in Half the Time*. New York: Warner Books, 1979. This is the book that got me started thinking about how to be more effective at my work. Not more efficient. More effective. In other words, doing the right things well, not just doing anything well. Worth at least 1000 times its cover price.

McConnell, Steve. *Rapid Development: Taming Wild Software Projects*. Redmond, Washington: Microsoft Press, 1996. Steve McConnell knows what he's talking about. I've used the method he describes in this book to run software engineering projects. It works. If you need to plan a project that involves developing a new product, use it. While it works for any kind of project, it may be the only reasonable way to plan the development of a new product.

Needleman, Jacob. *Money and the Meaning of Life*. New York: Doubleday, 1994. This book discusses just what the title says it does – intelligently.

Neihardt, John G. *Black Elk Speaks: Being the Life Story of a Holy Man of the Oglala Sioux, as told through John G. Neihardt (Flaming Rainbow)*. Lincoln, Nebraska: University of Nebraska Press, 2000. An Oglala Sioux medicine man's memoir. In it, Black Elk demonstrates a wisdom not shared by the people who almost annihilated his tribe.

Ouspensky, Peter. *The Fourth Way: A Record of Talks and Answers to Questions Based on the Teaching of G.I. Gurdjieff*. London: Routledge and Kegan Paul, 1957. A more discursive presentation of the ideas Mr. Ouspensky presented much more concisely in *The Psychology of Man's Possible Evolution*.

Ouspensky, Peter. *In Search of the Miraculous: Fragments of an Unknown Teaching*. London: Routledge, 1957. An account of Mr. Ouspensky's years of study with his teacher, G.I. Gurdjieff. The account also includes a fairly thorough discussion of the ideas he so concisely presented in *The Psychology of Man's Possible Evolution*.

Ouspensky, Peter. *The Psychology of Man's Possible Evolution*. New York: Hedgehog Press, 1950. An extremely concise exposition of The Fourth Way - a set of intellectual tools one can use to broaden and deepen one's understanding of one's place in the world. Thought-provoking. Mr. Ouspensky was a recognized authority on the theory of higher dimensions and higher states of consciousness.

Perls, Frederick J. *Gestalt Therapy Verbatim*. Lafayette, California: Real People Press, 1968. Available on the Internet at www.fritzperls.com/books. Transcriptions of actual sessions that Fritz led. Amazing demonstrations of what he could evoke from the people he was working with by simply directing their attention to parts of themselves they had ignored or repressed. The results are stunning.

Perls, Frederick J. *In and Out of the Garbage Pail*. Lafayette, California: Real People Press, 1969. Available on the Internet at www.fritzperls.com/books. This is Fritz's autobiography. He learned a lot. Read it, and maybe you'll learn what he learned with less suffering than he experienced. You'll be a much more contented person if you can do that.

Peters, Thomas J. and Robert H. Waterman. *In Search of Excellence: Lessons from America's Best-Run Companies.* New York: Warner Books, 1982. This is the book that introduced me to the idea of continuous improvement – never being satisfied, always working toward perfection, and getting everyone in the organization involved in the effort. A great book.

Peters, Thomas J. and Nancy K. Austin. A *Passion for Excellence: The Leadership Difference.* New Work: Warner Books, 1985. A continuation of *In Search of Excellence.* More inspiration for people who aren't satisfied with the quality of the work their organizations are doing. Read it when you're discouraged with how things have been going for you.

Peters, Thomas J. *Thriving on Chaos: Handbook for a Management Revolution.* New York: Harper-Collins 1987. This book finishes what *In Search of Excellence* started in 1982. It tells you how to do what that book suggests - in detail. Get it. It won't be easy to do what it tells you to do, but if you can, you'll accomplish amazing things.

Polya, George. *How to Solve It.* Garden City, New York: Doubleday, 1957. Dr. Polya uses high school mathematics to present a general procedure for solving almost any kind of problem. Brilliant. Pay special attention to the one-page list of questions at the beginning of the book. Asking yourself those questions can get you to the solution of almost any problem that confronts you.

Qigong. Start with Ken Cohen's book. It's listed in this appendix. You may not need to look for a teacher. One may find you. The Zen Buddhists sometimes say that if you're a sincere seeker after truth, Boddhisattvas will spring up everywhere to help you.

Ram Dass. *Be Here Now.* San Cristobal, New Mexico: The Lama Foundation, 1971. The classic. If you can do what he suggests in *Be Here Now,* you don't need to read this book. You're done.

Ray, Kali. *In the Flow with Kali Ray: Triyoga ® The Art and Science of Yogaflow®*. Los Angeles: YogaFlow, 2004. Kali Ray has made four DVDs that teach basic yoga practice: Free the Spine, Free the Hips, Gentle Cardio, and Strengthening. If you master the exercises she teaches in those four DVDs, your body will probably remain strong and flexible much longer than it will if you don't. She teaches gently, slowly, and oh so effectively.

Rogers, Carl and Barry Stevens. *Person to Person: The Problem of Being Human*. Boulder, Colorado: Real People Press, 1967. This book is an account of a personal journey. Barry Stevens finds her way to an understanding of her life and to deeper understandings of her relationships with her friends. Carl Rogers comments on what she says about her experiences from the vantage point of 40 years of therapeutic practice. Carl invented what he called client-centered therapy, a very effective method for helping people understand their experiences. It you're looking for a deeper understanding of your own experiences and more satisfying relationships with the people who matter to you, this is a book you'll enjoy.

Salinger, J.D. *Franny and Zooey*. New York: Little, Brown and Company, 1991. Franny's having a nervous breakdown. Her brother Zooey figures out what to do about it.

Satir, Virginia. *Making Contact*. Berkeley, California: Celestial Arts, 1976. Someone once asked Virginia to write a short summary of what she'd learned about person-to-person communication. *Making Contact* is the result. Short, sweet, wonderful.

Satir, Virginia. *The New Peoplemaking*. Palo Alto, California: Science and Behavior Books, 1988. Virginia was the genius who practically invented the detailed analysis of interpersonal communication (See *Making Contact* above.) If you want to learn how to raise your kids, read as much as you can of what she wrote, and get in touch with one of her students. If you want to learn how to raise yourself (Your parents may have made a few mistakes, and may not have finished the job.), do the same.

Schumacher, E.F. *Small Is Beautiful: Economics As If People Mattered.* Point Roberts, Washington. Hartley and Marks, 1999. This book makes the definitive argument for keeping things small and simple – in economics, in business, in government, and in life. Read it.

Shah, Idries. *Learning How to Learn: Psychology and Spirituality in the Sufi Way.* London: Penguin, 1996. Many people think they can just decide to learn something and learn it. Idries Shah shows you why that's not the case, and tells you what to do about it.

Sinetar, Marsha. *Do What You Love, and the Money Will Follow: Discovering Your Right Livelihood.* New York: Dell Publishing, 1987. A very practical approach to finding out what you were meant to do, and making your living doing it.

Stevens, Barry. *Don't Push the River. It Flows by Itself.* Lafayette, California: Real People Press, 1970. This book is a memoir of Ms. Stevens's experiences working with Frederick Perls during the last year of his life. It's very revealing of the way Fritz worked, which was a very effective way of helping people change.

Strozzi-Heckler, Richard. *In Search of the Warrior Spirit: Teaching Awareness Disciplines to the Green Berets.* Berkeley, California: North Atlantic Books, 2007. This is a fascinating book that demonstrates the importance of moment-to-moment awareness in the crucible of combat, where skillful leadership is crucial to survival and success.

Tai Chi. This is the foundation of all the Chinese martial arts. It's a beautiful art in itself. You'll need to find a teacher. Or perhaps one will find you. Look around on the Internet; search for "Tai Chi" in your local area - for example, search for "Tai Chi Philadelphia" if you live in Philadelphia. Evaluate the people you find the way I suggest in BUILD A PERSONAL SUPPORT NETWORK and CHOOSE YOUR TOOLS WITH CARE.

Toastmasters International. There's probably a club near your town. It may be the best place to learn how to speak in public.

Tolle, Eckhart. *The Power of Now.* London: Hodder and Stoughton, 2005. This has become a tremendously popular book. It explains how important it can be to be aware of what is happening in the present moment, both internally and externally. It doesn't explain how, though. Consult Girard Haven's *Creating a Soul* or Peter Ouspensky's *The Psychology of Man's Possible Evolution* and *The Fourth Way* for practical advice on the 'how' of being present – being aware of what's happening now.

Ueshiba, Morihei. *The Essence of Aikido: Spiritual Teachings of Morihei Ueshiba.* Tokyo: Kodansha International, 1993. Mr. Ueshiba invented Aikido. He was an honorable warrior for peace - he refused to train the Japanese army during its attempt to conquer Asia in the 1930s and 1940s. Read this book, and if what he says in it appeals to you, find a teacher. Try searching the Internet for "Aikido" in your local area. For example, search for "Aikido Chicago" if you live in Chicago. Evaluate the people you find the in way I describe in BUILD A PERSONAL SUPPORT NETWORK and CHOOSE YOUR TOOLS WITH CARE.

Vitale, Joe and Hew Len Ph. D. *Zero Limits.* New York: John Wiley, 2007. This book will teach you how to use *Ho O Pono Pono* - a formula for transforming negative experiences into positive experiences. Who could ask for more?

Weinberg, Gerald M. www.ayeconference.com This is the website for the annual conference Jerry started in 2000 with a number of his friends – experts at facilitation, leadership, team-building, and project management. The conference is great. I wish I could have attended every one.

Weinberg, Gerald M. *Becoming a Technical Leader. An Organic Problem-solving Approach.* New York: Dorset House, 1986. You can download the book from several sites on the Internet. Search for it by title. Jerry also sells it as an e-book. Pay for it. It's the basis of a wonderful leadership workshop that Jerry has run for over 30 years. Attending that workshop considerably improved my leadership skills.

Weinberg, Gerald M. www.geraldmweinberg.com This is Jerry's official website. Browse around there. There's much of interest. Don't be fooled by the casual appearance or the plethora of material. There's gold in them thar hills.

Weinberg, Gerald M. *An Introduction to General Systems Thinking*. New York: Dorset House, 2001. Study this book to learn how to test ideas – yours and others'. If you apply the methods it presents you'll rarely go astray.

Weinberg, Gerald M. *More Secrets of Consulting: The Consultant's Tool Kit*. New York: Dorset House, 2002. More wisdom from Jerry about how to give and get advice. In this book he describes an intellectual and emotional toolkit that he contends will help you stay out of trouble when you're trying to help someone else solve a problem. Provocative, but (I think) less helpful than his earlier *The Secrets of Consulting* (described below).

Weinberg, Gerald M. *Quality Software Management, Volumes 1 through 4*. New York: Dorset House, 1992, 1993, 1994, and 1997. In my opinion, the definitive books on software engineering management, AKA how to lead highly creative technical people.

Weinberg, Gerald M. *The Secrets of Consulting: A Guide to Giving and Getting Advice Successfully*. New York: Dorset House, 1986. This book is full of insights into human behavior that will serve you well if you can incorporate them into your approach to leadership. Often funny, always helpful. Enjoy.

www.livingpresence.com. This is the website of the Fellowship of Friends, a school for people who are trying to learn how to live in the present moment, rather than the future or the past.

www.yelp.com. So far this is the best referral site I've found on the Internet.

Yoga. This is what you need to study to maintain flexibility and strength as you grow older. Good yoga teachers abound. Search the Internet for "Yoga" in your area. For example, search for "Yoga San Francisco" if you live in San Francisco. Evaluate the people you find the way I suggest in BUILD A PERSONAL SUPPORT NETWORK and CHOOSE YOUR TOOLS WITH CARE.

Zannos, Susan. *Human Types: Essence and the Enneagram.* York Beach, Maine: Samuel Weizer, 1997. This book explains the most precise system I've found for classifying people by essence type – the type they were born to be, not the type that they were programmed to become when they were growing up. When trying to predict how someone will behave under stress, their essence type is the type you want to know.

CHAPTER INDEX

www.ingramcontent.com/pod-product-compliance
Lightning Source LLC
Chambersburg PA
CBHW072025190526
45166CB00015B/506